This book is dedicated to
Gloria Jean

LEARN THE ROPES... AND WIN WITH

BOLD MONEY

"An easy-to-figure book on options trading. Even if you don't plan to play the market, it's a good read."

—New York Daily News

"An excellent choice for rookies seeking a like-it-is introduction to a fast game."

—Kirkus Reviews

"Options trading can be fun. And this book's a good way to get started."

—Seattle Post-Intelligencer

"A good beginner's tool for the average investor."

—Booklist

"A refreshingly irreverent look at the world of options trading."

—Chicago Tribu

MELVIN VAN PEEBLES

BOLD MONEY

HOW TO GET RICH IN THE OPTIONS MARKET

WARNER BOOKS

A Warner Communications Company

WARNER BOOKS EDITION

Cover design by Mike Stromberg

Warner Books, Inc.
666 Fifth Avenue
New York, N.Y. 10103

A Warner Communications Company

Printed in the United States of America

This book was originally published in hardcover by Warner Books.
First Printed in Paperback: January, 1987

10 9 8 7 6 5 4 3 2 1

CONTENTS

ACKNOWLEDGMENTS

I would like to express my immense gratitude to Ted Hayes, who, in his position as consultant, was instrumental in bringing this book to fruition. As my colleague, Mr. Hayes's dedication and expertise were invaluable to this undertaking from inception to completion. It is also a pleasure to acknowledge my debt to Mary E. Nowlan, who adopted this venture as her own and who poured endless hours and boundless enthusiasm into these pages. I am grateful also to David Vigliano, the editor who offered me this project, and to the publisher, Larry Kirshbaum, who championed the idea of a populist, "user-friendly" primer on options.

Down on the Street, first and foremost I am hugely indebted to Dr. Henry Jarecki, who led me across the bridge into the world of finance, and to Roger Geissler, incisive guru extraordinaire. Thanks and appreciation are due Hartman E. Blanchard and Mark Miller, who applied their years of experience and savvy as traders to reading, critiquing, and rereading this manuscript. My gratitude to Tom Russo, amicus curiae, and Stan Lefkowitz, amicus humani generis. Thanks also to Robert J. Brody and Joseph L. Conway, who graciously lent their expertise in reviewing the manuscript in progress. Notwithstanding all the help from my friends, advisers, and assistants, named or anonymous, the buck stops here. Any errors or omissions are solely mine.

FOREWORD

This book is devoted to the Options Game and how to make it work for you. It is a primer designed to guide you through the mysteries of the market. (Incidentally, if this book helps to improve the caliber of your game lifewise, don't be surprised, for the philosophical parallels are amazing.)

You will learn what options are, how to determine the risks and rewards, and how exactly to go about the buying and selling of options. You will learn how to choose a broker and to handle him, how to supervise his navigation through the murky waters, and how to maximize his skills. (Remember, you are the captain. It is your ship, your money, your fate. The broker is only a mate.)

Financial success is an old-fashioned pirate tale with the rubies and pearls of success sleeping in an option trading treasure chest, waiting, just waiting . . . for *you*. First, of course, the map! To ensure the gods' benediction and your success, the four hidden clues of the map (The Mists of Moolah, The Game, The Gauntlet, and The Odds) must be mastered and made to reveal their secrets unto you.

BOOK I

THE PASSAGE

1

THE MISTS OF MOOLAH

So you want to be wealthy! Fair enough. Poverty, even modest poverty, is undeniably a burden. Some people even find it un-American . . . or anti-Christian. Whatever your reason, you are clearly someone interested in making money, since you have already taken the first step by picking up this book. Well, keep reading, for you have come to the right place. This book is intended to open up to you the secrets of the options market and show you the way to become rich from the comfort of your own home through the purchase of options.

Who should trade options anyway? Many more people than you have been led to believe. Yes, there are other roads to riches, but they are not as accessible to the ordinary person in the street, to John or Jane Doe citizen. If you are not a rock star, a stellar athlete, or an inventive genius, or whatever, options are for you. If you are not well connected to begin with, but count among your virtues fortitude, tenacity, and normal intelligence, options are for you. If you enjoy pitting your sense of the future against the crowd and crossing swords with the mob, options are for you.

Luckily, options can be fun. (It's a good thing, too.) The voyage to a better life is seldom a short or easy one. You are going to need all the Stamina, Concentration, and Sense of Humor you can muster. Remember . . .

". . . You gotta let the trip itself be half the joy of the going there," the hobo proverb goes.

There will be trials and tribulations and, as they say, ". . . times that try men's souls . . ." But as you see the faint of heart falter and fall by the wayside, you will learn to appreciate the true nature of the obstacles in your path and grow to understand that they are only friendly challenges that test and strengthen your resolve. Once you have clambered aboard your ship and set sail for the rainbow, once you have the deck of determination planted firmly beneath your feet and the rudder of destiny nestling in your palm, life will take on a vivid intensity. You will feel a surge of triumph and exhilaration as you clear each reef, ride each wave.

I am not of the Iodine School of thought that says if it burns it must be good, that if it hurts it must be helpful. On the contrary, you comprehend better and are more effective and efficient if you enjoy as you learn. In this book we will cover the practical, necessary things as pleasantly as possible and without condescension or dealing in baby talk. I have made an effort to discuss each subject with the simplest possible terminology that clarity will allow. (I bristle when I read pseudo texts that contain unnecessarily complex language, writing that is more designed to impress and intimidate than instruct.) If you are hoping to be, or need to be, bamboozled, this is not the book for you. If you want clear explanations and plain analogies, if you want to succeed at trading options, if you want to get the maximum power out of your money and make your dollar holler, not just give some itsy-bitsy squeal, then this is the book for you.

Once, in high school, rushing through some supplemental assignments on my own, trying to keep up by staying a little ahead of the pack, I ran into a math problem that I couldn't get to come out right. I tried and tried, diligently checking my figures over and over, but I couldn't get my numbers to coincide with the answer at the back of the book.

Frankly, the teacher was a monster and I didn't want to expose my delicate ego to his sarcasm, so I went to my best friend, who happened to be one of the smartest kids in the class, and asked for his help.

"Look," I said, "I took the square root," etc., etc., and I enumerated my steps while he listened patiently.

We worked the problem out together, and lo and behold, he arrived at the same number I had.

He was as afraid of the teacher as I was, so we took our problem to *the* smartest guy in the class. "Look, we took the square root," etc., etc., my friend explained, launching into the problem. The smartest student listened carefully, applied his own meticulous calculation, and lo and behold, came up with exactly the same answer that we had.

The three of us were in the lunchroom discussing our next move when the class oddball overheard us. "Can I give it a try?"

"Sure!" we agreed.

"Look," began the smartest student in the class, who was now acting as spokesman for our little group, "we took the square root . . ."

"Hold it," Oddball said. "Don't tell me."

We were puzzled.

"Don't tell you?" my buddy said. "Why?"

"We're simply trying to save you the boring part," I added.

"Look, guys," Oddball said, "if you tell me what you did, I will never see it for myself. I'll just step into your line of thinking. Let me study it for a few moments, OK?"

Oddball retreated to a corner with a ham-and-cheese. We waited. I remember it as if it were yesterday. The two class geniuses both had chili dogs and I had a bologna sandwich.

Oddball came back with, lo and behold, the right answer. Was it magic? NO.

In questioning him, we retraced his steps and found that I had misinterpreted the basic question and the other two guys, following in my shoes, had not picked up my fundamental mistake. I had made a zig when I should have made a zag.

There were a number of morals in that high school math episode for me. For one thing I was appalled at how easily an error can slip into posterity. If the correct answers had not been in the back of the text to refute my figures, I honestly doubt if I would have ever questioned if I was right. Moreover, it taught me not to go off half-cocked, for it doesn't matter how well intentioned the motive or what meticulousness follows the first steps; if the beginning assumptions are poorly formed (that's polite for wrong), the rest cannot come out right. "Look before you leap," tis true . . . strive for an overview before taking the plunge . . . study the forest before you venture amongst the trees.

Speaking of overview, when I came to the gates of Wall Street and took a few paces back to survey my new home, I was dumbfounded by what I saw. A kind of perennial fog or cloud shrouded the kingdom! Furthermore, none of the scurrying citizenry incessantly inhaling the fumes seemed to be aware of the vapors.

To this day I am still struck by the sheer strength of the Wall Street mystique, a permanent cloud of mythology, a toxic fog, a hallucinatory mist, that permeates everything. They breathe it, they believe it, they preach it—but they don't see it. The truly amazing—the believe-it-or-not—part, is that no one seems to be aware of its existence.

Even though this cloud of mythology affects how one thinks and therefore how one does business, I have never seen it listed as a trading factor (the closest mention I ever found was to its primitive cousin, Rumor). Even in the most scholarly Wall Street treatises and texts delving into every component of trading from the basic to the esoteric, even among descriptions of supply and demand, liquidity, marginal utility, volatility, etc . . . nary a word!

Nowhere do the **MISTS OF MOOLAH** (since I discovered

it, I get to name it, right?) swirl more thickly than around the Options game.

Three sources intermingle to create the befuddling MISTS OF MOOLAH.

The Aging Process (Wall Street is no spring chicken).

At their beginnings, institutions, like people, are flexible, adventurous, and open to change, only to coagulate as time goes on.

Success (Losers don't have a vote on Wall Street).

Winning inflates the head and breeds pomposity while simultaneously constricting the mind with fear of falling from grace. On the one hand, the triumphs of the past are lionized, but on the other hand, they are desperately scrutinized for clues to prolonging the lucky streak.

Danger (Wall Street is a high-risk industry).

The greater the hazard, the greater the rigidity. The constant peril fosters an unconscious yearning for stability, and since that is not possible in trading per se (flexibility is at a premium), the craving for permanence must be "projected," as they say in psychiatry, or transferred elsewhere—to the architecture, for example, to the solid marble columns; to the ponderous phrases inscribed over the doors of the various exchanges. And most of all, it is transferred to and through the mythology.

You have seen the HOW, the origins of the MISTS OF MOOLAH. The WHY, their importance, is obvious. Still, let's take a brief look before we move on to the WHAT.

Hardening of the overview, sclerosis of the Big Picture, is epidemic in the financial industry (Hallelujah and Yea, team), and therein lies a major advantage for our side. If your opponent is fuzzy, you clearly have an edge on him—right? And getting the edge is what Wall Street is all about. The edge is what you must search for continually. The Mists provide a sense of well-being, but at a price. That reliance on the clouds can be turned into a plus made to work for us. The MISTS OF MOOLAH are everywhere permeating everything Wall Streeters do. Hard to believe but true.

The aberrations caused by the Mists are legendary. For example, Wall Streeters insist that what they do be called "speculation," not "gambling." Gambling seems a reasonably rational and certainly natural pursuit, since life is a gamble in the first place. Nobody guarantees when you step off that curb that you are going to make it to the other side. Anyway Moolahnites detest the word. The dictionaries say:

Webster's New Collegiate

GAMBLE	to play a game for money or other stake
SPECULATE	to enter into a transaction or venture the profits of which are conjectural or subject to chance

Scribner Bantam English

GAMBLE	to risk something of value for possible profit

SPECULATE to engage in a risky business venture in the hope of making big profits.

The contorted hairsplitting Wall Street argument goes: To gamble is to assume a risk for the risk's sake, whereas to speculate is to assume an economic risk that would exist normally. The only real difference as far as any fool can see is that speculating gets a few larger words and a longer explanation in the dictionaries. But Moolahnites are adamant on the subject, and if it gets them through the night to classify themselves as speculators, I guess it's all right. At any rate, gambler versus speculator is only a ludicrous symptom of breathing the MISTS OF MOOLAH, which is the Moolahnite preoccupation with status.

All Moolahnites believe to varying degrees that theirs is a sacred calling, that they perform a public service. They are afflicted with a great need to feel that they are doing the "important" or "right" thing, preferably both. (It doesn't stop anyone from cutting anyone else's throat, however.) Their rationalizations for making a buck are endless: free world commerce, price discovery, adding depth to the market. On and on they are obsessed with having a guilt-free but weighty position in the universe.

"Forewarned is forearmed," "Don't get sucked in," "Delusions can be costly." Despite what Wall Street PR would have us believe, it does not follow that since fried chicken makes for good eating, trading Colonel Sanders stock is oiling the economy. (Placing a bet at a racetrack window isn't a vote for democracy.)

* * *

The truth, dear friend, is that if you wish to make the world a "better" place, you cannot do it directly through the trading of options. You can, however, make a pile of money, and the only thing money can't buy is poverty. Always remember that if your goal is to elevate the condition of your family or aid your fellowman or get a Rolls-Royce or two, you are in a better position to do so standing on your own two financially solid feet than splat on your back.

The MISTS OF MOOLAH have a darker side, a more pragmatic, sinister function beyond dim-witted self-righteousness. The clouds shroud the seething avarice and flimflam the competition, to whom misinformation is usually dispensed in the guise of "conventional wisdom." The more lucrative the business, the more conventional wisdom is available . . . and this brings us back to options. Nowhere are the Mists thicker or the advice quicker than around the Options Game.

Much of what will be said in this book will fly in the face of "conventional wisdom." As a rule, I have found conventional wisdom usually to be a euphemism for *convenient* wisdom—convenient for someone else. Most conventional wisdom ends up keeping you in a low income bracket. Good deals are whispered, not shouted. If everyone is willing to give you advice, there is usually something in it for *them*. Be suspicious! Check it out . . . everything . . . everyone . . . even me!

Why am I giving you all this good info so cheaply? Is it because I have a heart of gold as big as all outdoors? Er, no, not really. I am writing this book, giving you these pearls because I receive a percentage of the sales. If the information is good, the book sells. If the book sells, I make money . . . Volumewise . . . Otherwise, I would charge you more than the price of this primer to divulge the truth.

Conventional wisdom has it that you need at least a tiny fortune to deal in the market ". . . say, a hundred thousand dollars in the bank and at least forty thousand liquid to play with, before you should even consider getting into the Options Game . . ." etc., etc. Conventional wisdom optionswise implies that the table stakes are so high that the little guy cannot possibly play the game. That's a lie.

There is a way to play the Options Game without a fortune, a way they don't tell you, a way to play in which your restricted capital, instead of causing you to lose any advantages, can actually be a plus for you.

First, let's take a preliminary look at options to find out what they are all about . . . at what they are and what they do.

2

HARVEY'S BIG TOE

What does an option do? Is it voodoo? Well, options actually do have a wondrous magical ingredient. That fabulous ingredient is called leverage. Using the magic of an option's leverage of one hundred to one (100:1), you can grab the chance for that Big Score. Through leverage you control more of an object than you could afford to purchase outright, so much more that a small price change can mean a big profit.

Naturally, such an explosive potential is a Pandora's box unleashing torrents of sociopsychological tensions.

There is no more fitting beginning for a chapter on the meaning of options than the ending of a speech delivered by Dr. Henry Jarecki, chairman of Mocatta Metals Corporation and a leading figure in trading circles who is renowned for his tremendous financial knowledge, his business acumen, and his willingness to tell it like it is. Never were the questions and answers put more succinctly than in the paper Dr. Jarecki delivered at the Financial Times World Conference in Lugano, Switzerland, in the summer of 1983:

> In summary then, I believe that speculation derives from man's greed and his desire for stimulation and his desire to participate in the world's affairs and feel he is somebody. All of that taken together can of course lead to a disaster.
>
> There is, however, a solution to this disaster-prone need, and that solution is the option. An option is, as you know, the right but not the obligation to buy or sell and the market in such rights is one of the world's fastest growing markets. It provides the speculator with all of the benefits without any of the risks—except the cost. It gives him the stimulation and sense of participation and sense of being somebody and being free that he needs but it frees him from the disaster element and gives him a real chance, especially because the option provides the average person with staying power. He does not get called for more money and is thus not forced to close his position out or add money and fear what he has done.

No, you don't have to follow the convenient conventional Wall Street wisdom that if you are an average person in modest circumstances you should not speculate. OK, but how do you get from there, from "modest circumstances," to being wealthy? Options. Ready? Let's shove off.

* * *

You are probably not as naive (polite term for ignorant) as I was at the beginning. It is doubtful that anybody could be. Still, we will begin at the beginning, with definitions, sort of a review. (Don't be ashamed to go back over this section if you have to. Besides, nobody will know.) Moving from the metaphysical to the actual, just what are options anyway?

call option an option for the options buyer to buy an asset from a seller

put option an option for an options buyer to sell an asset

options buyer (holder) an investor who buys (pays a premium) for an option

options seller (writer) a seller who receives a premium for an option

options premium the price of an options contract (normally one contract controls 100 pieces; thus a $5 premium costs $5 × 100, or $500)

exercise price (striking or strike price) the price per share or other unit at which the holder of the option may exercise his option to purchase (in the case of a call buyer) or sell (in the case of a put buyer) the underlying asset

expiration date the date after which the option is no longer valued and the amount of time up to nine months ahead during which the option may be exercised

underlying asset the object on which an option is based

option a promise to meet the terms of a legally binding negotiable contract which for a price (the premium) gives the buyer (holder) the right, in the case of a call option, to purchase from the seller (writer of the call) for a limited amount of time (expiration date) and for a fixed amount of money (the striking price) an underlying asset. In the case of a put option the buyer (holder of the put) for a premium has the right to sell to the seller (writer of the put) for a limited amount of time and for a fixed amount the underlying asset.

Traditionally, the underlying asset has fallen into one of three categories: *commodities* (wheat, cotton, silver, gold, pork bellies, etc.), *financial instruments* (government and municipal bonds, mortgages, etc.), and *stocks* (ownership in various corporations, banks, television companies, auto manufacturers, etc.). It is currently possible to trade options in any of these categories.

The Moolahnites used to love to proclaim that options trading was a Serious and Vital link in the health of the Gross National Product. However, as the interest in options has grown, and the rivalry among the various exchanges for business has intensified, more games, increasingly abstract and difficult to explain away so sanctimoniously, have been invented. Today there are even options on options. For the moment, suffice it to say that the assets underlying an option can be almost anything—even apples.

One lazy Saturday morning two farm boys who lived near the Mississippi River decided to go fishing. Along their route, they spied a sign announcing an apple fair on the other side of the trees. The friends decided to have a look.

There were apples everywhere, packed in bushel baskets, stacked in crates. A horse-drawn wagon loaded down with bright red McIntoshes pulled up. Ned's and Harvey's eyes lit up, because McIntoshes, which made the world's best apple cobbler, were hard to come by that year because the climate hadn't been just right.

"How much for a basket?" Ned hollered up at the man driving the wagon.

"$2.00 a basket," the man yelled back.

"$2.00!" Harvey retorted. "Heck, that's pretty steep, Macs or no Macs."

"$2.00 a basket." The man's offer was firm. "I'll be here till six o'clock," he added.

Boy oh boy, if those McIntosh apples didn't look good, just sparkling under the midmorning sunshine. But both boys agreed $2.00 a basket seemed like a lot.

Already a small crowd was gathering around the old wagon asking prices. That was the way these fairs worked. During the early part of the day the sellers would set a price and hope people would pay it, but as the day wore on, the prices could go down or up, depending on the demand.

"They're beautiful!" Harvey said out loud.

A stranger who had come to the wagon replied, "Yep, but I seen better."

"Better?" chanted Ned and Harvey in unison. "Where?"

"Not here yet, later though. They gonna come in this afternoon from Beechum County. Prettiest Macs I ever did see," he confided softly. "Better wait."

The stranger moved on. But the more Harvey watched the people buying those Macs, the more he thought he'd better get 'em while the gettin' was good. He fished in his pocket for his money.

"What are you doing?" asked Ned. "You heard what the man said."

"But what if it rains and that load from Beechum doesn't make it, then what?"

"Rain!" Ned guffawed, looking up at a clear blue sky.

"My big toe says it's gonna rain," Harvey replied, wiggling his left big toe.

"Big toe or no big toe, I'm willing to bet that we'll be able to buy those same apples come six o'clock for $2.00 a basket or even less."

"But if it rains, the ferry from Beechum closes down. Then those Macs could even go as high as $3.00 a basket and there is no way I can pay more than $2.25."

"Never on your life," said Ned authoritatively. Then, thinking he'd show off to Harvey just how smart he was and make himself a profit to boot, he added, "I'll tell you what. I'm willing to bet that when we come back past here after fishing that them Macs won't be selling for more than $2.00 a basket."

"My big toe don't lie," Harvey insisted.

"Well, put your money where your mouth is," Ned challenged. "You give me a quarter as belief money in your big toe, and if when we come from fishing they are selling at $2.00 or less, I get to keep your 25 cents. But if them apples are selling for anything over $2.00 a basket, I'll buy 'em myself at whatever that price is and sell them to you for $2.00 a basket."

Harvey, never being as fast with figures or schemes as Ned, had to stop and think a minute.

"You mean," Harvey repeated, "if they are selling for two bucks a basket or less, then you just get to keep my 25 cents? But if those apples are selling for more than $2.00, you'll buy 'em at whatever price and sell 'em to me at $2.00 a basket guaranteed?" Ned practiced his used-car salesman's smile for Harvey, who replied, "Well, if I give you this 25 cents and them Macs is up, I don't care how much, I'm gonna give you $1.75 and—"

"$2.00," Ned interrupted, correcting him. "That 25 cents can't be applied against the price. That's mine no matter what happens!"

"Well all right, then," Harvey agreed. "I suppose that's fair, all things considered. $2.00 then, but as sure as the day is long, I'm gonna call on you to keep your part of the bargain."

"No problem," Ned said, checking the sky again. "That's what your 25 cents is buying you, the right to call on me to keep my promise to sell you those Macs at $2.00—nothing more—even if they go sky-high, over $2.00 a basket."

Harvey thought about it. The midmorning sun just kept climbing higher in the sky, but his big toe seemed to be aching a little bit more.

"OK, you got a deal," said Harvey, handing over a shiny new 25-cent piece to Ned.

Heading for the fishing creek, Harvey asked Ned, "How did you ever come up with that idea anyway?"

"Read about it in a book about options," Ned bragged.

"Op . . . what?" remarked Harvey.

"Options," Ned said. "Since I'm planning to be a rich man someday, I always keep up with the latest goings-on."

"Huh?" said Harvey.

"Simple, Harv, for just a quarter you bought the right to purchase those Macs at $2.00 a basket. And since I'm the one you paid your money to, then I'm the one who sold it to you. So you just bought yourself what they call a call option."

"So I just bought myself a call option, did I?" Harvey mused.

"Yep," said Ned, coolly fingering his newly acquired 25 cents. "Yep, I sold it and I get the premium."

The boys walked on in silence for about a mile.

"Ned, guess what," Harvey chuckled.

"What?"

"My big toe is talking to me again."

Do you follow so far?... the MacIntosh apples are the underlying asset. Suppose the underlying asset is stock in the XYZ Pharmaceutical Company, and a researcher there invents a fountain-of-youth pill. Overnight the stock would zoom upward. The value to the holder of call options would increase while the value to the holder of put options would decrease. If, on the other hand, poison was discovered in one of XYZ's products, the stock, underlying asset, would plummet and the value to the put holder would increase while the value to the call holder would decrease.

Harvey paying his quarter (the premium) made him the call options buyer (the holder), and Ned taking the twenty-five cents made him the seller (the writer) of the option. The two dollars Ned guaranteed as the price to furnish to Harvey the basket of Macs is the exercise price (striking price), and the expiration date is the time when they return to the apple fair on their way home from fishing.

Back to the boys.... Who guessed correctly? Only the future tells.

Heading homeward several hours later, the two friends turned the bend toward the apple fair.

Dark clouds had gathered but they hadn't felt a drop of rain. The old horse-drawn wagon with the McIntoshes had just about sold out.

Ned, eager to hang on to his 25-cent premium, made his way straight to the grizzled old farmer.

"How much for a basket?" he yelled up.

"$4.50 a basket."

"Come again?" Ned hollered, sure that he had heard wrong.

"$4.50 a basket," the old man shouted back.

"They were $2.00 a coupla hours ago."

"Yep, but they're $4.50 a basket now," the grizzled farmer said as he filled an order for three baskets from a fat man and his skinny wife.

"Wasn't there supposed to be some Macs coming in from Beechum County?"

"Yep, but early this afternoon it went to raining cats and dogs over there. They closed the ferry down."

$4.50 a basket. Ned winced to himself.

"You promised!" Harvey said, looking Ned square in the eye. "A deal is a deal and I want my apples."

"Last basket!" the wagon seller called out to the half dozen people still milling around the wagon.

"Okay," Ned grumbled, "I'll . . ."

Just then a pretty red-haired girl spoke up. "I want 'em," she screamed.

"Well, I only got one basket left," the farmer said.

"I'll pay $5.00," the girl offered before Ned could get a word in edgewise.

"$5.00, okay," said the farmer cheerily, starting to hand the basket to the girl.

Ned had to offer $6.00 to honor his deal.

The girl was determined. "Six and a half," she shot back.

"Seven!"

Harvey watched in amazement as Ned and the girl bid that basket of apples all the way up to $10.25. He'd never seen anything like it before.

A clap of thunder struck so loud that the old horse started getting skittish.

"$10.50," the girl said.

They had drawn a crowd and Ned saw plainly that if he didn't beat out this old red-haired girl his reputation as an upcoming tycoon would be severely damaged.

"$10.75," he shouted.

"Tina, that's enough," a stern voice cut through the excitement before the girl could raise Ned again.

The young lady stopped bidding and reluctantly followed her father toward their old pickup.

Just as the grizzled old salesman handed Ned the basket of apples Harvey got the strangest idea.

"Oh, excuse me, folks," Harvey called, running up to the redheaded girl and her father.

"I saw you back there, miss, and I thought you was real good."

Her father flashed a tobacco-stained grin. "Yep," he agreed, putting his arm around his daughter. "They don't grow 'em much tougher than my Tina here."

"Well, I might be able to get a basket of Macs for you"—the words stuck in his throat—"for $10.50."

"What?" she said.

"$10.50," Harvey repeated, not knowing whether to say it again or turn tail and run.

"I'll give you $10.25, okay?" said the girl.

In less than two seconds Harvey had run off

and was back again with the apples Ned had just paid $10.75 for.

"Here." He pushed the basket of Macs at her.

"Okay," she said enthusiastically as she counted out $10.25.

Ned and Harvey lumbered toward home.

"I just can't believe it," Ned explained. "What you did, Harvey Johnson, was lower than a snake's belly."

Harvey seemed not to pay his angry friend much attention.

"Lower than a snake's belly," Ned repeated.

"Well, fair is fair," Harvey said finally. "When I bought that er, op . . . er . . ."

"*Option,*" Ned finished the word for him.

"Yeah, option, well, you said that you was guaranteed to sell them Macs to me for $2.00. That's what I paid the quarter premium for, that guarantee. You didn't say I couldn't turn around and sell them again."

"Not only did you buy my $10.75 basket of apples for $2.00," Ned snapped, almost unable to control his anger, "but you sold them for an $8.00 profit!"

"That ain't the point, Ned," said Harvey.

"Well, just what is the point, then?" Ned snapped back.

"The point is you should have never bet against my big toe."

Is the picture optionswise clearing up a bit?

Originally, long, long ago (in fact, human nature being as mischievous and meddlesome as it is, it realistically probably lasted not more than a week—or the time it took someone to figure out a diverting perversion), options were used solely as insurance against the slings and arrows of outrageous fortune, as a hedge against potential calamity lurking in the whimsical fluctuations of the market value of something or other. Let's go back to an example in thirteenth-century England. A weaver gets an order for five tapestries for the duke's castle. He's happy but worries that suppose in the spring the price of wool, ten bucks (or its equivalent) last year, goes up on him to say twenty, eating up his profit. Prudently, he would decide to reduce his profit, by the cost of a call option. He would go and find himself a Ned (a seller) to whom he would pay a premium that the seller would negotiate, in exchange for a guarantee that he could buy wool in the spring at not more than ten dollars.

That's how options began. But the lure of an "unknown," the siren song of a market's fluctuation, was too fertile a territory in terms of both entertainment and excitement to be ignored and left to such mundane activities as serious business. Speculators stepped in, and down through the ages options as a form of simple, dull, original "risk transference" was joined to options trading as a game.

Slowly, through the years, the variations on the trading of options multiplied. The first innovation was speculation on both sides of the fence. Not just a seller who guaranteed the price would initiate the trade but the buyer, too. No longer was it just the tapestry maker but some guy who thought the price of wool was going to go up and he could make a killing if he could locate a tapestry maker.

The years have flown and the Options Game has grown . . . strategies piling on top of strategies, innovations on top of innovations, interest in options trading attracting players in ever-growing numbers and ever-increasing size, pension funds, corporations, private portfolios (Moolahnites adore each new latest innovation, which they subconsciously see as daring and which they have a tendency to succumb to, whether it is suitable for them or not).

We, on the other hand, shall stick to one of the two original basic options strategies, not because of any antimodern philosophy, but because it is simply the best strategy for the modest investor. With a clear-eyed understanding of what you are doing, the disadvantage of limited capital can be neutralized. Because options are versatile tools and many strategies, such as hedges, spreads, rollovers, and conversions, are available does not mean that those strategies must be used. Beware! If a tool exists, it does not follow that it must be employed. Surely, you may question, if options have this versatility there must be some good to be derived from these tools. True. For example, there can be advantages to certain defensive tactics if you have a substantial enough fortune to defend. On the other hand, there are strategies that would be ill advised because they are too costly or involve a time lag unless you are a trader on the floor itself.

You can go to the racetrack with several hundred dollars and spread it around willy-nilly, and perhaps you'll luck on to something, but if you choose the right horse, you only need two dollars to be a winner. The strategy we will use is more suited to a sniper with a limited amount of bullets (read "dollars") than someone with a machine gun. If you don't know how to shoot, you need the machine gun. But if you can use a rifle accurately, if you understand trajectories and just what each bullet can do, a sniper's rifle can be just as deadly and much more cost-effective than a machine gun. Let's pick our horses carefully.

Make leverage work for you. Take advantage of an option's fabulous ingredient the only way you can: Buy options.

But *ONLY BUY. DO NOT SELL.*
ONLY BUY. DO NOT SELL.
(This is not a typo. This is a truth.)*

Forget the "versatility," the big-time fancy "portfolio instrument" stuff. Don't get sucked into seeking to try to duplicate the sophisticated glamorous strategies of the Wall Street big boys. The truth is, anytime you *sell* an option, other than one you already own (all the sophisticated strategies require that you do), you must meet a margin requirement: leave money in a quasi-government escrow account to ensure you can cover your commitment, which freezes a substantial amount of your operating capital.

Options may seem confusing at first glance with theories being rattled off a mile a minute, but remember, money matters usually originated in some logical premise, to facilitate some real-world need. And the trick in understanding is to go back to the beginning.

The Options Game, just like Rome, wasn't built in a day.

*Only sell when you are liquidating a previously purchased position.

3

JUST LIKE ROME

In the beginning a couple of cavemen grunt, gesture, or whatever they did back then, and finally finish by exchanging a spear for a piece of fur. This transaction was the great-great-great-granddaddy of trading, the origin of Wall Street. Options trading today is the culmination of centuries of refinements on that spear-for-fur swap. The truth about options is buried in that evolution. The truth, they say, can make you free—maybe—but at least it will give us a leg up on the competition.

Trade is the machinery of commerce lubricated by human instinct. Human instinct in business has two sides, the greedy-quest-for-excitement side and the loathing-for-sticking-one's-neck-out-taking-chances side.

History is the past as written by the winners. The

beauty of the history of trading is it is only the winners that we are interested in anyway. The facts speak for themselves. It doesn't rightly matter whether you believe Moolahnitewise that the evolutionary "steps" to options trading were preordained rungs of some cosmic ladder or that the steps were sophisticated reflex actions akin to the ones that lead the blind sand mole to finding its insect quarry.

Anyway, back to the two cavemen and the pelt-for-spear incident. Shortly thereafter in the development of civilization we get to the part where tribes band together to build some common area, maybe a cooking room, altar, or animal pen. This group activity, in which everyone had an emotional or practical interest, was the forerunner of corporate shares.

Down through the centuries, people have worked out increasingly complicated ways of identifying, protecting, trading, and selling their interests. It was not long, jumping a few millennia, before merchants were combining their gold to build pools of money to grubstake caravans and cargo ships. The gathering of resources to do some project, too costly to do individually, was one of the two major forms of activity that became cornerstones of the kind of trading which eventually grew into Wall Street.

The other significant trading factor that became a cornerstone was risk transference. Risk transference has been around since before antiquity, since farmers struggled to protect themselves against the unknown, to buttress themselves against the fates of some capricious god who, feeling out of sorts, might cause a drop in the value of their crops between planting and harvest time.

The legacy of these two factors, the "organization of capital" to facilitate business and the "transference of risk," flourished and eventually led to the phenomenon known as Wall Street. Elements borrowed from these roots were incorporated in the invention of the Options Game.

Organization of capital, its accumulation, and its subsequent investment are fairly familiar to the general public. However, the layperson is less conversant with the concept of risk transference, although it is not difficult to fathom.

The need for risk transference was the origin of futures trading. Futures, as the word implies, consists of betting on the future. A futures speculator bets on metals that don't exist yet or haven't been dug. He bets on the delivery, the weight, the need, and the consumer desire for animals sometimes not even born and on crops not sown, let alone harvested. The net result is that one party, the producer of the commodity, hedges his risk and buys peace of mind by entering into a contract to sell his product at a discount based on a guesstimate of the value at a future delivery date to another party. That other party speculates that he can make a profit by agreeing to take the risk on the value of the commodity in the future. The Egyptians were rumored to deal in futures along the Nile, and futures were dealt with in Ethiopia around 1000 B.C.

In a very easy analogy, let's say a farmer is planting a crop, but he doesn't know for sure what the price will be for that crop when he brings it to market. What with floods, droughts, and locusts he feels that he has enough risk just sending it to market without having to worry about what he can sell it for once he gets it there. He figures out a price that he can live with and then tries to find someone who is willing to guarantee him that price. He enters into a commodity futures contract. To make a long story short, a commodity futures contract is an agreement by the seller to deliver a particular good on a particular date at a particular price.

To be more specific, let's say our farmer is a Babylonian or Assyrian in antiquity, raising whatever it was they raised back then (for purposes of illustration let's call it wheat). He knew he had to put out so much money for planting and so much money for feed for the oxen that had to plow the field. Calculating all of this, it came to \$7 (local currency, of course). He hoped he could get \$10 a sheaf, after harvest, when he got it to the mill. If it cost him \$7 and he sold it at \$10, he'd be making a \$3 profit. Not bad, he would say. But suppose the price went up and he was able to sell at \$12 a sheaf. Instead of making \$3, he'd make \$5 for his labors . . . well and good . . . terrific! But suppose, just suppose, that the gods weren't with him, and wheat went down in price and was selling at \$9, even \$8, a sheaf. His profit would be drastically diminished or, if wheat fell even further, maybe completely eliminated. Now, that's a big risk for one man to shoulder all year, plowing out there in the hot sun. So what would he do? He would find someone, a speculator, to step in to guarantee to buy it on the delivery in the future at a slight discount, say \$9.50 instead of \$10. The guarantor, gambling that wheat would be selling at \$10, would hope to put a 50-cent per sheaf profit in his burnoose. The farmer would be content, for 50 cents was worth it to hedge his bet. Sure, he would make less than what he dreamed for, but on the other hand, he was covered. The merchant that bought the contract would be pleased also, feeling his promise to pay $9.50 was a small risk to take for the opportunity of profiting 50 cents if it sold at $10 a sheaf, and even more if it sold higher. Of course, if it sold under $9.50, he would lose and wouldn't be too happy—but them's the breaks.

By the Middle Ages futures dealing was an idea whose time had come. In the Orient rice futures were in existence, and futures markets were rather commonplace at European fairs. In the eleventh and twelfth centuries dealers would meet with customers and discuss goods that would come by the next ship or caravan. Remember Shakespeare's *The Merchant of Venice* and *The Volpone* by Molière? In 1570 in England a year-round trading center was established, called the Royal Exchange of London.

In olden days the futures market dealt mostly in commodities, but the field has grown with the passage of time to include such diverse entities as mortgages (sold as securities), foreign currency, and other man-created entities grouped under the heads of favored instruments.

Although futures and options have many of the same elements in common, they are far from the same. I personally have always viewed futures as a primitive Options Game. On one side you have speculators, the traders and investors who buy the contracts and assume the risk (gambling for the potential profit) or the people who need the commodity for their business. On the other side are the hedgers themselves, the producers, the farmers, for example. Futures have leverage because when the speculator buys a contract he only puts up a percentage of the money, as a sign of good faith, until the delivery of the product. The good news is that the percentage can be minuscule (in fact, back then sometimes only a handshake, although handshakes soon proved to be undependable), but even today the margin requirement (money to show good faith) can be as low as 5 percent of the contract value. The bad news is that if the product shrinks in value while the speculator awaits delivery, he must immediately make up any difference in the contract value or lose his original investment. This enormous risk or the possibility of it deters many potential players. *Voilà!* That's probably why someone invented the Options Game.

Just when each game began is hard to say. Of course, the further back you look, the more difficult it is to disentangle one starting point from the other. Nevertheless, one thing is certain whether you go back to the Ethiopian origin or four thousand years ago to China, as some believe, or to the caveman: Auction markets, with the rise and fall of emotions, the excitement of the participants, have been with us a long time, and whether they deal in slave girls, spears, beavers, fish, gold, securities, futures, or options, they are all more or less the same.

What is clear, is that by the seventeenth century Holland had begun to develop the stock market as we know it today. The first known book on the market was written in 1688 by Josef Penso de la Vega. The English title was *Confusion of Confusions*. Appropriately, de la Vega commented on the confusion, or seemingly confused activity, of the auction markets. He noted that there was a great deal of sharp dealing and cheating going on. Most Wall Street observers will say that in today's market this is no longer the case. That's true. In recent years dishonesty has been drastically reduced (not, however, for reasons of mankind reaching a plateau of higher moral development, but because of legislation, standardization, and technology, important factors we will cover at length in a later chapter).

There is little in existence today stock-marketwise that did not exist in at least some rudimentary form in seventeenth-century Holland, including embryo clouds of delusion and hypocrisy that began moving in to engulf the trading scene. For even back then tiny MISTS OF MOOLAH were forming to obscure the truth, the philosophy being that lucrative affairs best be disguised and hidden. As Ambrose Bierce was to observe over two centuries later in his masterpiece of iconoclasm, *The Devil's Dictionary*, "The gambling known as business looks with austere disfavor upon the business known as gambling."

By the time de la Vega wrote his book there was an exchange operating every afternoon in Amsterdam, and there were open-air markets on Woomat Street and on the curb in the city's Church Square. Also, a new game had appeared, a game that would take another three hundred years to reach maturity, our game, options trading.

What a fascinating dichotomy human society is, with its propensity for compartmental differentiation (and its ability to simultaneously hold opposing views). Fascinating, too, are the contorted bridges the mind constructs to span the gap between the two views . . . but even more fascinating are the differences between two brains observing the same scene. On one hand, you have de la Vega recording the noise and double-dealing:

> The shouting followed by insults, the insults by mockery, the mockery ending in hand shakes . . . the crowd applauding the betrayals and quarrels:

And on the other hand, Adam Smith offers the ultimate Moolahnite apology (*Wealth of Nations*, 1776):

> Every individual endeavors to employ his capital so that its produce may be of greatest value. He generally neither intends to promote the public interest, nor knows how much he is promoting it. He intends only his own security, only his own gain. And he is led by an INVISIBLE HAND to promote an end which was no part of his intention. *By pursuing his own interest he frequently promotes that of society more effectually than when he really intends to promote it.*

In our pursuit for wealth never lose sight of the fact that money at the very best is only a secondary acquisition. The greatest riches are always in the mind, the perception of life that lies between your ears. Without the ability to marvel at the intricate, be it ever so simple, you are a pauper. Pure acquisitions, unless controlled, can be a vampire relentlessly sucking one's ability to be enchanted, leaving a jaded, bloated, barren shell. Mike Todd, the famous impresario, once said poverty is a state of mind. Personally, I was a rich man (in spirit anyway) from the day I said I was going to succeed or die trying. *Important:* I did not tell myself I am going to *try,* therefore I shall *succeed.* That would be self-blackmail. The implicit message of try-therefore-shall-succeed is (if I do not make it, I did not try) simplistic at best and potentially devastating psychologically. No, one's striving must be an integral part of one's success. It's not how many times you get knocked down that counts, but how many times you get back on your feet. In short, please don't lose your way striving for the treasure chest.

Enough philosophy. Back to Amsterdam, where the Options Game, in its infancy, had already created the biggest scandal (almost toppling the Dutch government) the financial community had ever seen (an omen of more sub-rosa behavior to come).

Fittingly enough, it being the Netherlands, the cause of the scandal was—can you guess?—tulips! Tulips, for heaven's sake?

Tulip bulbs were a hot property in the early seventeenth century, and tulip options were all the craze. Dealers would sell tulip bulbs for future delivery based on options to buy at a fixed price, call options, granted them by growers. If growers were nervous about the minimum price, they could in turn buy puts from the dealers. Everyone was rushing around adjusting his exposure to suit his vision of acceptable risk. (Options were then, as they are now, especially useful to growers as a hedge against unfavorable fluctuation.) Everything seemed rosy (or should I say tulipy). However, there was one weak spot, a little loophole in the formula, a "little loophole" that incidentally would plague options for another three hundred years. The loophole tulip-bulb-wise was that there was no organization to insure that everyone would honor his option commitments. With no rules, no framework, there was no way to know if anyone would fulfill his contract, since there were no margin requirements to keep a speculator from ruining the grower as well as himself.

In 1636 the market suddenly dropped. The writers of puts—that is, speculators who had taken a premium from the farmers and in return guaranteed to pay a good price for the tulips even should the price of tulip bulbs go down—were wiped out. Actually, more to the truth, the majority of put writers simply disappeared into thin air, having never had any intention of paying off if the market went against them. This default, in turn, had a domino effect and many farmers were ruined. There had been no previous financial disaster even near that magnitude. The Dutch economy wavered on the brink of collapse, and the world was having its first big-time business catastrophe. The Provincial Council at The Hague was called on to solve the problem and restore market credibility. The council came up with the genius solution that contracts should be honored . . . nice idea but unenforceable. As someone must have said, it is as difficult to get blood out of a tulip as out of a turnip.

The unsavory reputation of options did not improve with the passing of the years. Options from their inception were and still are the most versatile and flexible of the trading tools, a fact not lost on the disreputable low-life types in the financial community who set about concocting schemes to use them as vehicles for bending or completely circumventing rules. Options had such bad press that they were banned in England by the Barnard Act of 1733. Notwithstanding the embargo, options were so useful they continued to be traded illegally in Great Britain until 1860, when the ban was lifted. They were outlawed in England a couple more times, once in the 1930s and again during World War II.

Options, during their early history and until recently, have been linked with some shady deals in the good ole U.S. of A. but never banned. George Washington in a letter circa 1773 said, "Gambling is the child of avarice, the brother of iniquity and the father of mischief." He was not referring specifically to options, but he would have felt the glove fit.

> The distribution of wealth . . . depends on the laws and customs of society. The rules by which it is determined are what the opinions and feelings of the ruling portion of the community make them, and are very different in different ages and countries; and might be still more different, if mankind so chose.
>
> **John Stuart Mill,**
> *Principles of Political Economy,* 1848

Anyway, despite our Founding Father's view, Charles Lamb's eighteenth-century observation that "man is a gaming animal" was to prevail.

In 1790 America had its first stock exchange in Philadelphia. By 1792 Wall Street itself was in the midst of a boom. Merchants, forever on the lookout for business opportunities, kept small batches of securities which they sold over their counters like calico or pickles. That is where today's Over-the-Counter (OTC) market got its name. Options trading, to put it mildly, continued to have a troubled childhood. Nevertheless, the big metamorphosis that would catapult options into their present preeminence was drawing nearer and nearer. One tainted options scheme after another kept surfacing. Unscrupulous brokers pushed questionable stock deals on unsuspecting clients and took rebates in the form of options on the stock of the company that they sold to the customers. Scandal followed scandal. But "it's an ill wind that blows no good," they said, and a gentleman named Russell Sage, working on a scam to avoid the usury laws, created the modern puts and calls.

At any rate, options survived it all. Then, finally . . .

On April 26, 1973, the Chicago Board Options Exchange (CBOE) opened for business, and suddenly it was a new ball game. Options came of age in one fell stroke. Through a brilliant blend of old, new, and borrowed elements the trading of options was revolutionized and transformed from a useful but tawdry trading tool into a reputable, reliable instrument.

Some old-style OTC options still exist, but they are dwindling, while CBOE-listed options have grown at a prodigious pace, beyond their biggest boosters' wildest dreams.

What is so great about the CBOE options anyway? In retrospect, it all seems, as most truly profound things do, so obvious, so simple.

Standardization of striking price, as against a limitless amount with OTC.

Standardization of expiration date. Listed options expire on the third Friday of the month. This reduced the time from roughly 250 days to 12, which simplified record keeping for all parties and made surveillance easier.

Creation of a clearinghouse, the Options Clearing Corporation (OCC), which guaranteed the performance on the contract and simultaneously eliminated the necessity for buyer and seller to meet.

In short, the CBOE narrowed the variables in options trading down to one factor, the cost of the option itself (the premium), and they all lived happily for ten years (that's almost forever in Wall Street time). Then just as it seemed the last wrinkle had been invented, someone pulled a new options rabbit out of the hat and *voilà!* there was another game, one that, as they say on Madison Avenue, is destined to revolutionize the industry.

The Moolahnites have always piously maintained that what went on on the floors of the exchanges was trading, not gambling. They claimed that Wall Street with its Price-Discovery thesis . . . et al . . . was the finger in the dike, the barrier between civilization and the Dark Ages. Options equal gambling? . . . Heavens, no! Quite the contrary, options were the oil to enhance the underlying assets' flexibility. The role of options was to add versatility to portfolio management, etc., etc. Butter would not melt in their public relations people's mouths, options being tied to the underlying assets, you see, which is useful for commerce in discerning the annual rainfall at the base of Mount Kilimanjaro. Blah blah blah or something. Then *shazam* . . . Suddenly this new game appears without, as they say in pornography, "redeeming social benefit."

The new game is called Index Options—options not on underlying assets, be they securities, commodities, or financial instruments, but *twice* removed from that. Index options are predicated on the gambling which in turn is based on the gambling about the fluctuation in the futures market. Of course, the Moolahnites have been working overtime to come up with a rationale, some portentous apology. In the meantime everyone has jumped onto the new bandwagon with both feet.

In the words of the Wall Streeters, "Indexes are what's hot these days." Hot is usually defined by the growing numbers of investors trading (and these numbers can be reflected in the open-interest figures which are to be found in your local newspaper's financial listings). So why are these options indexes so hot? Probably because indexes are simplistic, a nice easily grasped concept; they represent a basket of stocks, sometimes a narrow-based basket—a grouping of only energy-related companies, or only transportation businesses, or only high-technology industries—but sometimes they have a broader base. Indexes reflect the trend of the entire segments of the market rather than individual stock performances. And oh yes, there is a potential 18 percent tax benefit over traditional options.

In March 1983 the Standard & Poor's 100 Stock

Options Index was introduced. Through September 1985 the average daily volume of stock options traded was 239,874, which was almost as much as the daily average for all of the 145 individual stocks traded on the Chicago exchange.

Now I put to you the statement that "the world is a fickle place." I'll even go one step further: "Failure is an orphan but success has many fathers."

Listen to this. In the column "The Striking Price" in the March 7, 1982, issue of *Barron's,* the weekly financial newspaper, the writer indicated that the new S&P (or CBOE 100) Index (made up of such stocks as Eastman Kodak, AT&T, Exxon, GM, and IBM) was due to start trading the following Friday but was being shied away from by pros, because of questions relating to time lags and differences in settlement prices and a lot of other concerns that only the knowledgeable pros have the insight and cleverness to discern.

In the March 21, 1983, edition of the same paper in the same column by the same writer, Dean Witter's Macon Brewer noted (with 20/20 hindsight, if you will) that "the CBOE options appeal to the mass market." The CBOE volume of 8,427 on the second day of trading had topped the combined action for the day of the ten most recently added options, including treasury bonds, the New York Stock Exchange Composite, and foreign currencies.

On January 15, 1985, the *New York Times* said that in 1984, 66 million S&P 100 were traded on the options exchange.

Now, ladies and gentlemen, a word from the pros who doubted the success of the CBOE 100 around

March of 1982. "What are you talking about?" says the pro indignantly to the interviewer. "We never doubted the success of the CBOE 100." And furthermore, he grins, wiping the egg from his face. "Why, just the other day I was telling my wife how I had predicted that those CBOE 100 options would go on to become the hottest thing in options. ". . . Yeah, unhumm, sure, Mr. Pro . . . yawn . . . what else is new?" Remember what I said about the father of success?

All right already, enough memory lane. It's time to go down to the Colosseum and size up the lions and the Philistines. We have peered through the Mists, thumbed through the history, taken a sniff inside the machinery. Now let's go climb through the ropes and check out the turf of the investors, the go-betweens, the speculators, dreamers, and schemers. . . .

4

IN THE FAR CORNER, WEIGHING . . .

Welcome to the floor of AMEX, the American Stock Exchange, a mecca of the Options Game. Don't mind the deafening din (the shouts and yelling won't subside until 4:10, when the market closes). That din is the sound of money changing hands, the most primitive noise in nature, even more elemental than the ocean's roar. Everywhere you turn there is a clock, symbolizing your fortune, stretching from the next second to sometimes nine months hence . . . the impending moment, the goose with your golden egg, or the hatchet for your neck. Old clocks with sweeping hands and late-model digital clocks, bringing whatever fluctuation of the market they will bring. Time, your opponent or your friend, your stairway to triumph or your elevator shaft to disaster, both destinies delivered by the same number on the clock . . . the following minute.

Rows upon rows of video screens, stacked two or three high, are arranged wagon-train style in circular clusters around the floor. A video screen is a flattened rectangularized version of ye olde crystal ball. Groups of traders, anxious suitors, your rivals for the market's affections, stand staring into the video screens mesmerized by the blips and flashing numbers hoping to discern a pattern that will reveal Lady Luck's next move. One glance at the furrowed brows and premature gray heads will banish any submerged fears of trader invincibility.

There stand your adversaries, with their entourage of alternately fawning and bored clerks, reporters, and runners, shifting uneasily from foot to foot with the trader's lament ringing in their ears.

Buy and you'll be sorry
Sell and you'll regret
Hold and you will worry
Do nothing and you'll fret.

Anyway, upstairs on the balcony of the AMEX with the huge trading floor stretched out below, the size of two football fields stuck together, one is reminded of the Starship *Enterprise* preparing for an attack by the dreaded Klingon Empire. The multitude rushes here and there, forms melt and re-form anew. The tides of destiny rise and fall, sweeping the fortunes of empires along. The bedlam beneath your feet is not an act for TV or an intellectual abstraction, but reality! A reality so firm you can reach out and grab it, or get grabbed.

The zoological maxim "Ontogeny recapitulates phylogeny" has recently come into dispute, but as far as stock exchange architecture goes it is certainly still true. The stages of evolution the AMEX went through can be clearly seen in the design of the trading wall. Even today, despite extensive renovation and massive modernization, traces of the exchange's rough-and-ready beginnings can be plainly seen, a prime Exhibit A architectural example of the MISTS OF MOOLAH tendency to enshrine history. The more uncertain the undertaking, the more desperate the search for some sense of order and stability. The prices flash across the screens with unrelenting regularity, changing constantly. Just to survive, let alone prosper, one must have great flexibility. Their perception of the world and of themselves, having solidified long ago, now passes from generation to generation resisting change. . . not without reason, I might add. (But more of that in a couple of paragraphs.)

In the beginning (Constantinople and New Amsterdam included) exchanges were merely outdoor auctions. A makeshift platform was set up in the middle of the road or alongside the curb. Clerks would hang from the windows of the buildings flanking both sides of the street and shout information to the traders below. When "real" exchanges were built and business moved indoors, what could be more "natural" than to have tiers constructed at each end of the floor to simulate the setup from the good ole days of the clerks hanging out the windows. To the present, notwithstanding telephones, tapes, and video screens, clerks in the tiers still gesticulate, shout, scream, and pass signals by hand to the traders below, just as their counterparts did outdoors more than a century ago.

In the foyer of the members' lounge adjacent to the cafeteria there are photos on the wall showing the early days, when lampposts were originally installed on the floor (when the exchange moved indoors), to recapture the feel of the outside. Those lampposts evolved into the present-day cluster, or "posts," of video screens that dot the floor, each post trading in a specific item, just as was done outdoors.

Besides Moolahnite nostalgia, the members of the exchange and their backup teams on and off the floors have other normal Moolahnite reasons, self-interest and greed, to revere the good old days and bemoan change.

The party line of the exchange—that the floor trader is there for the public good, making the marketplace safer by insuring continuity, liquidity, and stability—is a rather recent concoction. Off the record, many of the members are more candid. I have often been told, "Damn the public, I'm in it for the profit, man," or "I'm out for nothing but the dollar, you dig" (many people feel obliged to try to speak ghettoese to me). Anyway, originally, exchange members were not created as public servants, nor did anyone feel the need to tout them as such. They were just fellows making a living. As late as the turn of the century, if you wanted to trade stocks on the Curb Exchange (the forerunner of the AMEX), all you needed were good lungs and someone you could talk into letting you have an order or two. No dues, just nerve. Naturally, in such a frontier atmosphere the public was viewed as so much fresh red meat. But as public participation in the market increased and the "little privileges" the various exchanges granted to their members grew into indecent opportunities to fleece the public and make huge bucks, the government stepped in.

Most exchange members, the foot soldiers toiling in the golden trenches, fall into one of three categories: brokers, traders, or specialists. Of course, many of the members on the floor are the tip of the iceberg of a back-room team computing, calculating, and planning strategies. Never mind—back-room team, downstairs gang, upstairs crew—don't worry, as they say in the service, "They step into their underwear one leg at a time just like you do."

There are "commission brokers," who execute orders for brokerage houses or clients. There are "two-dollar brokers," free-lancers who carry out the difficult orders for commission houses and help commission brokers whenever they become too busy.

As to "the specialist," he functions in four ways. He is an auctioneer-cum-umpire, and since the Stock Exchange is basically an auction, his is a pivotal position. He has the option of a stock assigned to him, and all business conducted in that option, buying or selling, must go through him. He can also trade "on his own," that is, for his own account, using his own money. For this monopoly, last but not least, he is required to keep an active and orderly market in his option. Theoretically, he tries to balance out the market. If a bid or offer comes in that is not at the market price, he "puts it on the book" (writes it down) and as soon as possible matches buyer to seller or vice versa. The theory often doesn't work that way. Richard Ney in his incisive book *The Wall Street Jungle* puts it this way:

> . . . The regulatory bodies of the Federal Government have failed to face the basic fault in the specialist's modus operandi—namely that there is a conflict of interest built into his function. He is meant to be the representative—in the key position on the Stock Exchange—of the public, but at the same time he gains his income by trading against the public. Theoretically, then, he must adhere to a golden mean. But it is one thing to preach the golden mean and quite another to achieve it. . . .

Lastly, there is the trader, the epitome of the market. Once traders acted with their own money, but now most traders are working with or for a firm. They may rent themselves out as two-dollar brokers, if the occasion permits, but essentially their job is to come to the floor to trade for their firm or for their own account. The motive is profit, and a trader survives by his wits and his willingness to take risks. Traders are entrepreneurs and buccaneers, short on urbanity, long on confidence, independent, and with a high opinion of themselves and their calling.

Once upon a time, in the good old days that they bemoan the passing of, the members of the exchange roamed with impunity feasting on herds of yokels. But now the saber-toothed trader is facing the same fate as his namesake. Not only have the yokels learned, but government regulations and technology have all but obliterated the floor trader's edge.

Now each trade that takes place on the AMEX is recorded and electronically monitored to keep everybody honest. When anything goes awry, there is a record. However, despite the noise and at first glance what might seem to be confusion, little goes awry. After all is said and done, the AMEX is an auction market with nearly two hundred auctions going on simultaneously. It is a business like Monte Carlo, Atlantic City, or Las Vegas, but still nevertheless a business. It is about buying low and selling high, doing to the other fellow before he can do to you. There is a saying on Wall Street that "it's not gambling if you're winning."

If you will accept my disclaimer, here is a corroborating view of the Wall Street species supplied by a financier friend of mine who visited me at the Stock Exchange. We were on the balcony.

ME

(looking down; philosophically)

Ah, Wall Street . . . what is its raison d'être?

[Yes, I know I didn't have to say it in French. I could just as easily have said, "reason for its existence," but my friend wears a cape and is a very erudite fellow and I was trying to hold my own.]

FRIEND

(deadpan)

They have to put all those guys someplace and the jails are full already.

The gangster Lucky Luciano, on visiting Wall Street and having the system explained to him before his deportation, is reputed to have complained bitterly that he had joined the wrong mob.

The era of the saber-toothed trader is fading fast, and the exchanges as cozy clubs run for the benefit of the members is drawing to a close. The trader must now match wits on near equal terms with the public entrepreneur off the floor. In short, the "honor" of being a member is not as attractive as it used to be.

In order to have the honor of becoming a member of the exchange, little more is required than the money to buy a seat. "Seat" is a wistful misnomer, since there are no chairs on the trading floor and less opportunity to use them even if there were. The name carries over from the eighteenth century when traders used to sit while the president of the exchange would open the trading each day by going through the list of securities offered for sale.

Today a would-be trader must find someone willing to sell or lease him a seat. This is only a question of shopping around, since seats are always available for a price. The price varies with the enthusiasm and success of the market at any given time. Over the last twenty years, the price of a seat has swung back and forth from a low of less than $50,000 to highs of over $500,000.

Next, to become a member, an applicant must get two current members to attest to his character and must have his fingerprints checked to assure that he does not have an embarrassing criminal record and to make him more easily identifiable if he should acquire one. If all is well, he is given a quiz on the basic rules of the exchange. If he passes the test, he signs the book and he is in.

If he is a broker, he then has the right to charge a commission for the trades he executes. If he is a specialist, he gets to referee the game. If he is a trader, he now has the right to scavenge around the floor looking for bargains, pushing and shoving his way along the psychic roller coaster. His world becomes the gauntlet of premium price . . . the DMZ between a rock (risk) and a hard place (reward), a minefield of wasting assets. A kingdom where each tick-tock of the clock shrinks the option's time value. At maturity the time and time value finally converge on zero.

Hey . . . a crowd seems to be gathering over by XYZ. There must be some news. (Good? . . . Bad? . . . who cares as long as it's action!) Let's mosey a little closer and take a look-see.

"October 40 calls, 20 at 3¼!"

Did you hear that? Did you understand what the guy just said? He offered to sell 20 (contracts), October (expiration date), calls (type), at 40 (striking price), for a premium of 3¼ ($3.25).

"3 for 20!"

That other fellow just bid to pay him a $3 premium for 20.

Let's stick around a moment, something will probably happen. Why do I say that? Can I foretell the future? No way. Simple, it's the marketplace—a crowd means action. Action equals competition, competition means liquidity, and liquidity equals a narrower market. After all is said and done, the whole thing comes down to buying low and selling high. The *bid* is what a buyer is willing to pay, and the *offer* is what the seller is willing to part with his options for. The buyer and seller must agree on a single price or there is no deal. For the instant the spread (the difference between the bid and offer) is a quarter of a point. In other words, they are $500 apart. ¼ = 25 cents. .25 × 100 (number of stocks in an options contract) equals $25. $25 × 20 (the number of options) = $500.

"At 3⅛," the seller says, lowering his offer.

"Take 'em," another trader shouts, and the deal is consummated.

Time elapsed, maybe forty seconds. Number of times a day traders do deals? Zero to a couple of hundred. Size of deals? One option to a couple of hundred.

Who got the best of the deal? That brings us back to the future, those clocks with those inscrutable grins. Only time will tell. . . .

Traders like to keep their money circulating—they move in and out of positions many times a day. The cost of the commission if an outsider tried to trade that way would be prohibitive, but a member usually acts as his own broker and thereby avoids paying a commission. Of necessity at the beginning, then out of habit when they become rich, traders convert their paper profits for cash on which to live, whereas a part-time investor with supplemental income can take a more leisurely point of view.

Traders, whether they deal in stocks, commodities, options, or whatever, all do their business in one of three ways; there are technicians, fundamentalists, and intuitionists (or some combination). Technicians believe that the prices tell all, that price is king. At the basis of this belief is the conviction that market fluctuations mirror everything important to be known about a company. (The research done by the buyers of large blocks appears in the prices bid and offered; "discounted in advance" is the Wall Street expression.)

Fundamentalists, on the other hand, study the company itself: its management, the morale of its personnel, the state of its business, its capital reserves, its debt, and its past, present, and projected earnings, as well as its relationship to the other competition in the marketplace. This information is readily available from the companies' public reports or from statistical services, which offer a sort of *Consumer Reports* of trade.

While technicians study charts and fundamentalists study reports, the intuitive boys go by the feeling in their guts, usually augmented by anything from astrology to tidbits picked up in their roamings around the floor. But as they say on Wall Street, "Everything goes as long as it works." One trader swears he made three-quarters of a million dollars using the phases of the moon.

The members of the exchanges, the traders, brokers, and specialists, own the stock exchanges. The floor fellows are a prankish fun-loving lot, but the upstairs watchdogs are of the grim high school dean variety. The staff of the AMEX, including its president, are all technically employees of the membership. But from observing the regulatory body of the exchange which governs the activities of the members and for which the members universally profess scorn, one could get the distinct impression that it was the other way around.

Another quick glance backward into the heyday of the saber-toothed trader will explain the why of this topsy-turvy situation. After the debacle of the big Wall Street crash of '29 that pushed the country to the brink of bankruptcy, the federal government finally began to pay attention to the market's affairs. In 1934 the Securities and Exchange Commission (SEC) was set up to study the feeding habits of the members of the exchanges. Of course, the commission found fraud, duping of the investors, price rigging, and so forth, and also discovered that instead of being a stabilizing influence and a great boon to industry, as was claimed, the members of the exchanges tended to gravitate to the more volatile (active) stocks and would ride whatever trend was in the wind, in the process adding more destabilization than calm.

An in-depth analysis finally published in 1963, after twenty-nine years of research into the workings of the stock market, labeled the "Special Study of Securities Markets," proposed doing away with traders altogether. The government criticized the exchanges for operating with a rampant disregard for the public good. (Of course, the 1961 AMEX scandal two years earlier did not help the exchanges' cause much.) To save themselves, the exchanges swore to mend their wicked ways and promised to police themselves via the establishment of boards of governors who would monitor the behavior of their members. Jump-cut to the present day. The governing staffs of the various exchanges, created as buffers between the members' posteriors and the government's foot, and nudged by the SEC, take themselves very seriously and grow sterner with each passing year.

Well, that's it. The trader and his territory. The traders may brag, as they are sometimes prone to do, that they are unemotional to the core, have ice water in their veins, and are masters of clear thinking . . . sure, sure. One thing is very certain. Despite having roughly a half million dollars tied up in a seat and accompanying paraphernalia (equity, margins, graphs, annual reports, and/or rabbit's feet), the trader (he, she, or it) has no more assurance of what will transpire the next second, in terms of which way the market is going, than you do. In short, the guy over there in the far corner of the ring weighs in at about the same as you.

5

MOLASSES TO MICROSECONDS

Undoubtedly, the favorite American pastime is scheming on how to hit the *Big One*. Everyone loves dreaming about beating the odds, but few ever stop to reflect on the commission, the vigorish that the house takes for doing business. The commission has a direct bearing on how much of the pie you get to keep. Anyway, notwithstanding anything to the contrary, as they say in legalese, improved odds and lower commissions are the two reasons that options are a better deal today than ever before.

COMMISSIONS

Let's examine the lesser-known factor first. Two elements have substantially lowered the cost of doing business:

1. The CBOE
2. Modernization

ONE. When the CBOE was formed in 1973, besides the elements we examined in Chapter 3 (the standardization of striking price, standardization of expiration dates, and the creation of a clearinghouse), there was another big benefit to players of the Options Game. The cost of doing a transaction took a nosedive. Lower commissions set into motion a happy chain of events. The cheaper cost of doing business induced many new players, insiders and outsiders alike, into the Options Game, increasing volume and augmenting liquidity. The commission costs on CBOE-listed options are about one-half that of conventional options. Commission costs on the old-style over-the-counter conventional options necessitated that there be a big move in the stock before profits were possible. The lower commission costs on the CBOE allow buyers to profit from relatively small moves in the stock.

TWO. Modernization. The CBOE's streamlining of options through standardization was a giant step in the lowering of the cost of doing business, but an equally salient feature has been the mechanization, especially through electronics, of large areas of the day-to-day trading process. It would be difficult to overemphasize the impact electronics has had on trading, not just in lowering the cost of doing business, but in every other aspect of trading as well.

THE ODDS

Electronics brings us to the second reason why options are such a good deal today. Three elements have improved the odds for you:

1. Electronic price disclosure
2. Better governmental surveillance
3. Higher liquidity

ONE. Optionswise, the biggest bites out of your potential slice of the pie come from the cheaters, but electronic price disclosure (which gives everyone the availability of having the news of a buy or sell, the price, volume, etc., almost simultaneously) has, to put it bluntly, defanged the clubhouse guys with the borderline trading habits.

TWO. The enforcement power of the Securities and Exchange Commission coupled with government regulations, which are getting tighter and tighter in the public favor, has substantially reduced rip-offs of customers all along the trading process. Dishonest brokers, for example, once routinely engaged in churning accounts to fleece the uninitiated. Churning an account means inducing the customer to buy or sell unnecessarily for the sole purpose of generating a commission for the broker, regardless of whether or not the trade would be profitable for the customer. This practice has diminished significantly, but there are still blatant flare-ups.

The fabled leverage of options which can bring riches

beyond Aladdin's dreams does, alas, attract not only the good guys. Since options give a bigger bang for the buck and can't discriminate between crooks and the true blue, shady characters like insider-traders gravitate to them (an inside trader is someone who attempts to gain profit from information obtained under the table).

Thomas C. Reed, a former White House specialist on national security, was accused of trading with insider knowledge received from his father, a director of a company dealing in base metals. Reed was reported to have made a $427,000 profit on options in a period of forty-eight hours from an initial investment of $3,135. Leveraging power? . . . Pretty sweet odds if you ask me. That's just a peep at what the rewards can be if it turns out you have a good nose or big toe for the market, which, incidentally, unlike insider trading, is strictly legal.

Probably T. C. Reed's little detour would have gone undetected a few short years ago, but with the ability of computers to record and cross-check a staggering number of trades, fewer shady deals escape the routine daily muster. Although the situation is far from perfect, loopholes are being plugged methodically. A broker can no longer trade for himself *and* the public in the same option or stock, and furthermore, for a time the option and stock could not be billeted on the same exchange.

Electronics, which provided the wherewithal to rain on Reed's parade, have snowballed on Wall Street in the last three decades. For the record, technological innovation on Wall Street didn't just surface with push-button phones. As early as 1867 the automatic ticker system was introduced to disseminate sales, and in

1930 the system was running 500 characters per minute; by 1976, 36,000 per minute were being transmitted electronically.

THREE. With the increase in the action in the options market, and the subsequent rise in liquidity, the odds have improved dramatically. Increased liquidity came from the introduction and the success of a secondary market. The options buyer and seller were no longer tied directly to each other. Through standardization and the CBOE acting as an escrow bank, the buyer and seller had no need to meet and instead dealt with the Options Clearing Corporation established by the CBOE to act as a third-party guarantor. The new ease with which an investor could buy or sell brought more players into the game, increasing liquidity.

All the lowering of transaction cost and improving of the odds is fine. However, for our purpose the most important impact of all this liquidity, technological advance, and government scrutiny has been on actual value. Actual value must not be confused with the theoretical value of an option, which is computed by various formulas and is called real (or fair) value.

The actual versus fair alias real value squabble brings us once again to the cornerstone of the trading strategy of this book.

If you have been waiting for the other shoe to drop, for the book to get down to the hard part ("I thought options were so complicated"); if you have been feeling queasy experiencing a mounting uneasiness (if not downright guilt) as you sail smoothly page after page through the book without undue confusion, secretly asking yourself how can this be a serious tome if I understand what I am reading? Well, fret no more. Here we are, the tough part.

Gary L. Gastineau in his landmark book *The Stock Options Manual* says the key concept the investor must understand in order to make intelligent use of options is the *fair* value of an option. For the record, fair value is calculated on the basis of five factors:

1. Short-term interest rates
2. The relationship between the striking price of the option and the underlying asset
3. Time to expiration
4. The projected dividends on the underlying asset
5. The predicted volatility of the stock

Gastineau goes on to say that even though options evaluation is the focus of most academic options literature, the subject of *fair value* is rarely discussed in depth in books and articles that enjoy popular distribution. He feels that options evaluation is probably neglected by authors of most basic books on options for one or more of the following reasons.

1. The author does not understand options evaluation.
2. The fair value of an option is not the easiest concept to explain to the average reader.
3. It is easier to base options recommendations on stock predictions than to worry about whether the option itself might be over- or underpriced.
4. Actually calculating the fair value of an option is even more difficult than explaining the concept.

We are not going to devote much space to fair value, either (so much for the tough part), but not for any of the reasons on Gastineau's list. By the way, computer programs (welcome to the electronic age) now exist that will calculate fair value for you in the shake of a lamb's tail, and that goes for most of the other formulas of the trading game. So what do I have against fair value? Nothing personal. Am I trying to coddle/spare you? Nope. No. The reason we will not linger over fair value and other such formulas is not the availability of pocket Sonys, but because they tend to foster inappropriate priorities. They encourage us to take our eyes off the ball. In the liquid and technologically advanced market of today it is a redundancy, a diversion, and a needless drain on a small investor's precious resources to rely on formulas. The day of *real value,* for example, just like the prophecy foretold, has come, but it has arrived so quietly it has not been perceived. (Probably if it were observed, it would get the same shuffle ''denied and crucified'' as the last Messiah.) Let me break that down for you.

This brings us *kerplunk* right back to the cornerstone of our strategy, or, more accurately, to the premise on which that strategy is formed. The truth is that the mathematically gifted trader who was once able to stand on the floor of the exchange and make a profit simply by calculating in his head no longer has an edge. With computer usage a savvy ten-year-old can have the answer just as fast. The computer has made what was once a secret (at least for a minute or two, which is all it took to trade a fortune) into public knowledge. Through electronics there is a split-second flow of information to all concerned, not just to the fifteen traders within earshot, with the rest of the country getting the news later by horseback. With instantaneous dissemination to every exchange and brokerage house plus the rest of the world, from Tokyo to Rome to Akron, Ohio, with thousands of eyes watching every twitch of the screen, who is fooling whom? An option does not get out of line through mathematical oversight far enough to matter. And just suppose it did. Some trader on the floor would snap it up before you could get to the second digit of your broker's telephone number. Be of good cheer. I am coming to the silver-lining part. Look at it like this. Those guys scrutinizing the quotes and the opponents tussling in the dust for a sixteenth of a point are keeping one another and the system honest for us. What an open sesame technology and liquidity turn out to be. Through their combined wizardry we have changed our enemies, those avaricious, prehistoric traders, or, more accurately, pretechnological scavengers, into our allies.

There I was standing on the floor of the American Stock Exchange staring up at a July 50 call option premium trying to figure if I dared buy it. I, glancing down at the fair value, which I had secretly computed, suddenly had this revelation—WHAM—of almost biblical magnitude.

I was being seduced by the omnipresence of the system; the MISTS OF MOOLAH were getting to me. I had overlooked, ignored, been blind to the obvious. Hark, I was taking leave of my common sense. Wait a minute, I told me, realizing something was amiss. Luckily, I must have mumbled "fair value" aloud because the guy next to me announced his fair-value figure and the guy on the other side agreed. In fact, everyone in the crowd, it turned out, had the same fair-value figure, including me. Calculating something that is general knowledge is like going back to Stonehenge with a sextant to figure out what day it is today. Here I was surrounded by three ex-engineers, two from MIT, several assorted geniuses, and a bridge player tournament-class, not to mention through the magic of technology the rest of the world, from Hong Kong to Hamburg, all staring at the identical premium on identical screens. It dawned on me that the likelihood of discovering a fair-value bonanza was zero to zilch. Besides, if fair value was no secret, what was the big deal? What special edge is fair value if everyone knows it, and if there is liquidity *everyone* knows it. In short, if that premium had been out of mathematical kilter, someone would have pounced on it a couple of microseconds ago. By the way, that premise I was talking about is called the efficient market hypothesis. Also by the way, I bought the option. It turned out I was wrong, but not because of fair value. The president of the company drove his car off a cliff.

Anyway, technology has had the overall effect of narrowing the disparity between Wall Street and the public, similar to the role gunpowder played in upsetting the apple cart of the (serf vs. noble) feudal system back in the Middle Ages. Not only has technology assisted in lowering the odds and in sniffing out cheats, it has improved the sensitivity of John Doe's big toe; i.e., it can assist you in calculating your market moves.

* * *

Today's technology makes it possible to have a plethora of financial information, including options data, at your fingertips. For instance, with an attachment a home computer superior to the office computers that cost $75,000 and up fifteen years ago is now capable of talking with other computers (even internationally) via ordinary commercial telephone lines and can be purchased for a couple of grand. Operating procedures have been streamlined and the language simplified to make computers user-friendly. Still, as Krefetz and Marossi put it fifteen years ago in their book *Money Makes Money*, in a prophetic chapter entitled "On-Line Real-Time" about the bright future of computers on Wall Street:

> It is unlikely that computers will ever be put in complete control of investment decisions. Data processing machines are yet incapable of thinking for themselves and arriving at imaginative, intuitive, unorthodox, or in any way unusual conclusions. This is both their strength and weakness. They can only be as talented as their programmers and consequently the pervasive law of GIGO (garbage in, garbage out) has particular relevance to computers. . . .
>
> It is more than likely that the randomness of stock prices will be reduced. The market in J. P. Morgan's words "will fluctuate," but perhaps a lot less than before. In brief, the stock market will be more efficient, a truer reflection of real value.

Did you notice the term at the end of the last sentence in the quotation "real value"—i.e., "fair value," as in nothing new under the sun, just like they say? Anyway, back to technology and computers with their mind-boggling ability to crunch figures. The number-gobbling computer is a valuable tool, but beware! Achtung! Statistics and figures can only do so much. Sidney Weintraub in *Modern Economic Thought* voiced his reservations a bit more diplomatically: "The jury may still be out on whether mathematics, an incomplete language, can convey the variety of economic life in symbolic terms." However, whether you believe that statistics and figures can change the diapers or not, it doesn't hurt to be equally as armed as your opponent. "Better to have it and not need it than to need it and not have it" (School of Hard Knocks).

In short, at this moment in history, technology, in concert with lower transaction costs, governmental surveillance, and market liquidity, has dramatically improved the possibility of turning a profit optionswise. The odds look good. But (remembering that math-problem lesson I learned in high school) let's step back a second for an overview. Options trading is not the only game around. How about the odds in other ventures?

How about real estate? The U.S. Secretary of Agriculture estimates that forty thousand farmers, the nation's largest landowners, are mortgaged up to 70 percent of their still shrinking assets. In February 1985 fifteen thousand Iowa farmers marched to protest mortgage foreclosures brought on by plummeting land prices, which in some places are down 50 percent in eight years.

What about banks? The FDIC (Federal Deposit Insurance Corporation) reports a problem list of 889 banks. Seventy-nine banks failed in 1984 alone!

How about having your own company as an alternative? A recent Department of Commerce study sites that four out of every five new businesses fail to survive eight years, an 80 percent chance of failure, not to mention the time-intensive requirements of starting any new venture.

STARTING YOUR OWN BUSINESS

a. Putting the financing together 60 to 1

b. Making a go of it 4 to 1

The odds of doing any big deal are pretty slim. Here are some findings:

BUILDING A NEW INVENTION. One that sets the world on its ear enough to make you rich.

a. Getting it off the ground 20 to 1

b. Hitting it BIG 200 to 1

A HIT SCREENPLAY. As you probably can more or less guess, the Writers' Guild registers 13,000 scripts annually.

a. If all the movies were actually made from Writers' Guild scripts received (they're not) 50 to 1

b. Masterpieces 408 to 1

WRITING A BEST-SELLER. Out of the last one million books submitted only a few hit the best-seller list.

a. Of all books submitted 7,691 to 1

HIT SONGS. Of 125,000 copywritten annually your chances of getting a hit are:

1,300 to 1

LOTTERIES AND SWEEPSTAKES—you guessed it! These odds vary with the number of tickets sold but represent your chances on the average.

a. Sweepstakes	30,000,000 to 1
b. Lotteries	3,500,000 to 1

CASINO GAMBLING

a. Craps	100 to 1
b. Roulette	500,000 to 1
c. Slot machines	2,000,000 to 1
d. Baccarat	200 to 1
e. Keno	1,000,000 to 1
f. Blackjack	1,000 to 1

PERSONAL INJURY SUIT. Sure, why not? What's the chance of your hand or something accidentally getting caught in a door and you score for a cool million or more?

1,501 to 1

Here are a few other prospects. Of course, the downside risk, like Leavenworth or an early grave, can be pretty grim.

INSURANCE FRAUD. Some smarter and some dumber than you have lived to tell about it from a Caribbean island.

500 to 1

BANK ROBBERY. (Note: Tellers only keep at their station about $1,500 each.)

Making it to the door 3 to 1

COCAINE SMUGGLING

Outwitting Customs, cops, and rival gangs 6 to 1

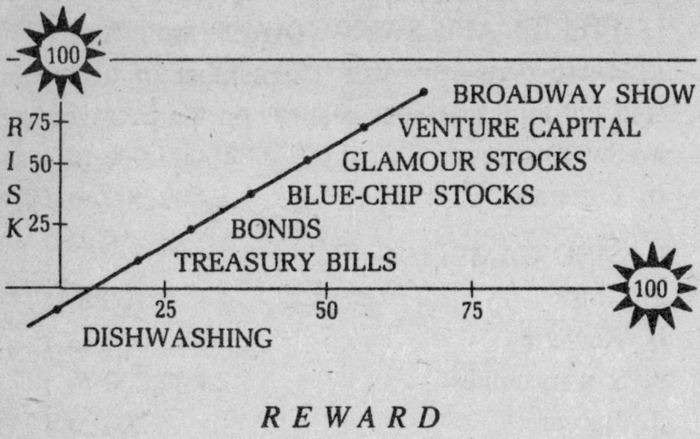

Life is not a fairy tale, and Wall Street is even less of one. You won't get something for nothing here, no Santa Claus, no Easter Bunny, no tooth fairy. Let's face it, when you put your hard-earned cash on the line, you are taking a risk. But without risk there is seldom reward. All those hard-bitten ole axioms are true . . . "It takes money to make money" . . . "No free lunch" . . . "No pain, no gain."

Okay. Now that technology has moved trading out of the slow-as-molasses age, and government regulations, listed options, and liquidity have pushed the market toward pricing perfection; okay now that minicomputers have made mathematical wizards of us all, solving complex calculations regardless of race, creed, or economic station, in miraculous microseconds; okay now that you . . .

Hold it, look!

"LAND HO!"

There! See, over there to starboard. There . . . on the horizon, that blue is our Treasure Island.

* * *

. . . I found it a pleasant journey and enjoyed your company. Congratulations would be a little premature since our trip is far from finished, but still, so far so good. But then again, on the other hand, that's what the man who jumped off the thirtieth floor said when he was passing the fourteenth.

. . . Speaking of jumping, the boat can't go any closer. We'll have to wade ashore.

Ready? It's not that deep, really. We'll leap together. One . . . two . . . three . . .

6

CHEST-HIGH

Right this way. Have we got an option for you! All kinds, any kind . . . you name it, we got it. How about something modern? The new line of index options are the closest things to automatic you'll ever see. Why in just a coupla years these beauties have swept the marketplace . . . who would have thought it? What a deal, too. Same basic advantages: limited risk and leverage. Plus—get this—a little tax incentive on any index if you qualify. The S&P 100 here is a sensational mover, bigger than all the options on the AMEX combined. We got franchises all over, service guaranteed . . . the New York Stock Exchange, the American Stock Exchange, we got Philly, in Chicago we got the Mercantile and Board of Trade, and out west the Pacific Stock Exchange. Look around, yessiree, we got options in gold, silver, soybeans . . . something foreign your meat? How about a deutsche mark currency option? Look, do yourself a favor and stay away from the narrow-based indexes. Oil, transportation, high technology, they're not moving so good just yet . . . and without liquidity where are you anyway. How about traditional? "Always safe with the tried-and-true," my mother used to say. You want options? Have we got an option for you! All kinds, any kind . . . you name it, we . . .

Seriously, car-salesman hyperbole aside, today is the best time since the beginning of history to get into the Options Game. Yes, there really are a multitude of options (models) to choose from. Plus the little extras, low commissions, good odds, and an efficient market doing most of your math for you.

Liquidity, plus electronics, plus government surveillance, plus trader greed, equals the efficient market hypothesis.

For the umpteenth time, the sensible, modest investor scenario is to *ONLY BUY.*

"Why?" Did you ask? "Why?"

Well, if you didn't, you should have.

Ask a thousand times if necessary. There is an old Slobovian proverb that goes "‡¢@*&8. %☆+"3•*@ /—#†©÷'5$#§-/®★○‡•0%;¢@™6," which means "Don't be ashamed to measure your cloth ten times because you only get to cut it once."

Buying of options is equal to an uppercut in boxing—maybe not so sophisticated, but it gets the job done better than anything else, provided you land on your opponent's chin. In the case of buying a call, this amounts to selecting a stock that is going up, and in the case of a put, selecting a stock that is going down. There is, of course, one more possibility and that is that the stock remains immobile. If a stock is listless and you feel it is going to remain that way, then pass it by. Yes, there are even strategies for making money from listless stocks, but none which would not entail having large amounts of your capital escrowed in margin accounts.

Why *ONLY BUY* options? Well, there are three reasons why *only buy.* Three? Yes, *three!* Other books will tell you there are *two*.

1. Your leverage, which can be tremendous.
2. Your risk, which is limited.

But there is a third reason equally important to someone trying to begin on a restricted budget, which is,

3. Buying does not demand additional money; only the premium and commission are required.

ONE, leverage. In every discussion I have ever read or heard about options buying it is always stated that it offers one supreme attraction to the investor, namely that it provides him a great deal of leverage. Leverage is tremendously important, but there is another advantage in options buying, one that is very attractive to a weak-kneed character like myself, namely limited risk.

TWO, limited risk. On the downside an options buyer is always safe: not sure, but safe. An options buyer can never lose more than the premium paid for the options contract. Just like a horse race, if the horse you bet on trips, breaks a leg, throws his jockey, or even dies coming out of the gate, you don't pay any more money . . . limited risk. You will have nothing to show for your money except the worthless stub rotting in your pocket, but on the other hand, you will not be called upon for more money. So it is when you buy an option. On the upside, theoretically at least, the potential to gain is unlimited. If the underlying stock on which you have bought your option moves in a favorable manner through the use of leverage, which simply means you control more stock than you have paid for outright, you are in a position to win dramatically, like a long shot at the track coming in. An option gives the buyer the right to purchase if it is a call or sell if it is a put a hundred shares per contract of the underlying security, at a stated price. If in the case of a call, for example, the stock rises past its stated price plus the premium and commission you paid for it, you are in a position to reap a profit by exercising your right to buy the stock at the lower price, like our old friend Harvey did with the apples, and then reselling at the new higher price. You will not actually do this because the commission to buy and resell the stock is prohibitive and can be avoided. It will be cheaper commissionwise and usually more profitable for you to simply sell your now-more-valuable call option. Speaking of cheap . . .

THREE, cheaper. It is incredible that the simple fact that buying is less costly is not shouted from the rooftops. (Oh, the pretensions of the Moolahnites.) And I don't mean 5 or 10 percent less costly, I mean 200,

300 percent and up! Buying a put or call is not as capital-intensive as selling one, since the law requires that when you sell you deposit more than 30 percent of the value of the underlying stock in escrow to ensure against possible default, a crippling requirement for the modest investor. Besides, of course, if you sell an option, all you can earn is the premium and your risk is unlimited. Weighing this, the peanuts of a premium against the unlimited risk involved, you have a sure scenario for disaster for the small investor. Options selling is a no-no.

We have seen why options are hot and buying is tops, so moving right along (here we are at the nitty-gritty, the big moment), let's explore the factors influencing the price of an option. Any textbook on the subject worth its salt will tell you there are four major forces. (Plus some minor determinants: the level of short-term interest rates and the dividend rate of the underlying stock.) The classic four forces are:

1. The price of the underlying stock
2. The striking price of the option itself
3. The expiration date of the option
4. The volatility of the underlying stock

Whoa! I submit that there is a fifth major force. A factor so obvious that it is continuously overlooked. (Forget the textbooks for a moment and think of detective novels, where the important clues are always right under your nose.) I am speaking of options themselves. Options are plural, not singular. What I mean is there are two kinds of options, puts and calls. Just to be on the safe side whadayasay we review them both.

To buy a call is to pay a premium for the right, but not the obligation, to buy something at a prearranged price. Okay, that's pretty straightforward and of course you remember our friends Ned and Harvey.

But a put is another animal. Something in our logic keeps bumping heads with the perversity of buying the right to sell. Let's take a look at the case of Percy N. Harris.

> Percy was famous for his uncanny ability to see any situation in its worst light. His detractors said that the "N" in his name stood for "negative." Anyway, Percy was a real estate salesman. Of course, being so negative his career was not flourishing. In fact, he was, as they say, in the process of being let go. On the very day that he was fired he overheard that the Woodhill section of town, a slum over on the east side, was scheduled for a major urban renewal from an unnamed philanthropist. Ole skeptical Percy didn't believe the rumor, but he realized that when the news got out, real estate values in Woodhill would skyrocket.
>
> So Percy gathered up all his savings, which happened to amount to $10,000. But instead of rushing out and buying a house in Woodhill at $10,000 before the news broke and selling it for a juicy profit when the prices rose, Percy decided to leverage his money.
>
> Percy took his $10,000 and bought a hundred washing machines at wholesale for $100 each. Within days of the rumor breaking, the average price of a home in the Woodhill section was at $50,000, five times its old value and still climbing.

Percy ran an ad in the newspaper offering a free washing machine to the first one hundred people who would agree to pay the purchase price of $50,000 if he could obtain a home for them in the Woodhill section of town within the next six months.

The citizens, fearing that prices would continue to climb and figuring how could they lose since they would get a washing machine for free, flocked to Percy's door. In less than two days he had his hundred contracts signed, sealed, and delivered.

In effect, as I am sure you realize, with the signing of each contract, Percy was buying a put option. The washing machine was the premium, the $50,000 was the striking price, and six months was the expiration date.

As time passed and more and more good news circulated as to how wonderful the Woodhill renovation was going to be, a new shopping mall, a library reopened, etc., and the property values continued to climb, Percy started to sweat. By carefully wording his contract he had the right but not the obligation to sell a hundred homes. Still he stood to lose the $10,000 he had paid in premium, i.e., the one hundred washing machines he had bought and given away.

Then it happened. The bubble burst. The renewal project was called off and real estate prices plummeted. To add insult to injury, the city decided to place its new sewage plant on a piece of ground they owned adjacent to the Woodhill section. Suddenly no one wanted to live in Woodhill and Percy was in the driver's seat.

One, Percy could buy up homes dirt cheap and force the signees of the one hundred contracts he held to live up to their obligation and pay him the full $50,000 per home he was entitled to, or *two,* he could allow them to buy out of their contract, liquidate his put, at a lesser sum. Since he was starved for operating capital, lazy, and I like to think a basically nice guy, he opted for the latter. Percy resold his puts for an average of $9,000 apiece making a little under $890,000 on the deal.

People started saying the "N" in his name was for "naturally smart."

A put may be perverse, but it can also be lucrative.

Anyway, getting back to the four classic major forces influencing the price of an option. They can be subdivided into two categories, the price of the underlying stock and the striking price of the option itself, which we can characterize with a little stretch of the imagination as the solid properties of the option. These two factors are the rock-bottom determinants of an options price. At Judgment Day optionswise—that is, on the day of expiration—they are the only factors that decide an option's value. The other two major influences of an option's price, the expiration date of the option and the volatility of the underlying asset, are more concerned with probability. That is where the gambling, I mean speculating, mainly comes in.

ONE, underlying stock. The underlying stock's price is the cornerstone of an option's value. Naked call buying provides an uncluttered illustration that the most important determinant remains the price of the underlying stock. That is from where, as they say in church, all blessings flow. Naked buying is the most primitive form of options strategy. (So straightforward, in fact, it can scarcely be called a strategy at all; naked means just that, unclothed, unprotected, without having a position in the underlying asset.) An investor might feel that a stock is going up. He does not own any of the stock, but he would like to cash in on his hunch. In that case he would buy a call option locking in the maximum price he would have to pay for that stock even if it should make an upward movement in three or four weeks, even months, whatever time forward it took as long as the time was less than the expiration of the option. Then when the underlying stock went up, he could simply sell his now-more-valuable option. He could also exercise his option and buy the stock at the cheaper price.

If you buy an option and the underlying stock does not stir, there is little to be done. Therefore, the selection of an underlying stock that is going to shift favorably is the most important choice the options buyer has to make. Next, once the stock that will move has been ascertained, the buyer should bring into play the second factor.

TWO, striking price. An option's striking price, which derives its importance from its position in relation to the price of the underlying asset, is the second most powerful determinant of an option's price. Buying an out-of-the-money option is usually a bigger gamble than an in-the-money option. What's out-of-the-money and in-the-money, anyway? The terms used to describe the relationship between the option's striking price (price at which the options buyer has the right to exercise the stock) and the stock's actual price are "in-the-money" and "out-of-the-money." Let's take a moment to review the connection between the stock price and the option cost. If the stock price is above the striking price of a call option, it is said to be in-the-money. If the stock is selling for less than the striking price of the call option, it is said to be out-of-the-money. Here is a call example: Stock XYZ is trading at $36 per share. The XYZ June 40 call option is out-of-the-money, because the stock is trading below the striking price of the option. On the other hand, the XYZ June 30 call is in-the-money because 36 is higher than 30, and a call option is in-the-money if the stock price is higher than the striking price of the option.

In other words, if all things remained the same until expiration date, the June 30 call would be a $6 bargain because you could buy the stock trading at $36 for $30, $6 less its market value, or $6 in-the-money. On the other hand, if all things remained the same until expiration date, the June 40 call would be $4 more expensive than if you bought the stock on the open market at $36. Why pay $40 when you can get it $4 cheaper—i.e., the June 40 calls would be $4 out-of-the-money. The cost of the option reflects in part its position to the striking price vis-à-vis the underlying stock. For a put, of course, being the right to sell, rather than the right to buy, the situation is reversed. If the stock is selling for more than the striking price of the put, it is out-of-the-money, and if it is selling for less than the striking price, it is said to be in-the-money.

An out-of-the-money option is a longer shot than an in-the-money option, and therefore, to entice you to take the risk, the relative cost is less. So the simple fact is that if the underlying stock moves dramatically, the out-of-the-money option will be relatively more profitable. Mathematically, there is less likelihood of a large move than a small move. Moreover, if the stock only shifts moderately, the in-the-money option, all things considered, may be the more profitable option. Normally, if the stock moves slightly, an in-the-money option will offer better rewards than an out-of-the-money one, but if the stock makes a large change, the out-of-the-money option is more rewarding. The premium for an in-the-money option is more expensive because the likelihood that the in-the-money option will expire worthless is smaller than the likelihood that an out-of-the-money option will expire worthless. Out-of-the-money options are sensitive to the volatility of the underlying asset because their major hope for profitability lies in a substantial change in the price of the underlying asset, whereas in-the-money options, which move almost point for point with the underlying asset, are more sensitive to changes in the interest rate.

THREE, expiration date. Time to expiration is also important when buying. The near-term option, especially if the stock is close to the striking price, will most nearly follow the fluctuations of the underlying stock and is the riskiest. An option can be viewed as a perishable stock. The long-term option—that is, the option with the most time remaining—on the surface has the least risk or rather more opportunity, but because it costs more it has less leverage and therefore a lower percentage of reward. Many people prefer to split the difference and buy an intermediate option. Pure premium price should never be the sole deciding factor in options buying. An amateur mistake many investors make is to buy the long-term option because it only costs a point or so more than the intermediate one, feeling that the extra price is a bargain for the three extra months of time. Rarely do options buyers hold their calls for more than forty-five to ninety days, so the three extra months go to naught, and even though it looks attractive it may prove to be unnecessary. At one time, the longer-term options were calculated with less scrutiny and it was easier to find a bargain lying around. However, with the intensification of interest in options in general, this opportunity has all but disappeared.

A tool sometimes used in choosing the best expiration date is to find the cheapest premium through comparison of premiums at a yearly rate called annualization. Figure out what you would be paying on a week-to-week basis. Say the premium is 2, and there are, let's make it easy, thirteen weeks left to expiration. First you divide the number of weeks in the year by the number of weeks left in the option: 52 weeks divided by 13 weeks equals 4. Then to get the annualized rate, you multiply the premium of 2 by 4, which equals 8, and that is your annualized premium, 8.

FOUR, volatility. The volatility of the underlying stock is very important in establishing the order of desirability of which option to buy. Sometimes the papers will make a glamour list of the best option buys, often based solely on percentage changes in the underlying stock—such a ranking misses the point and can lead to errors. Options on a nonvolatile stock will sell for less than similar options on a volatile stock because volatility increases the possibility of a large advance or decline during the lifetime of the option. If options are ranked solely on the percentage change in the underlying stock, the least volatile stock offering the cheaper options will appear to be the better buy. The beta rating of a stock is a helpful index of volatility. The beta is the degree to which a stock reacts to the state of the market. A stock with a beta larger than 1 has a higher volatility than the average. One is normal and less than 1 is sluggish. To determine the volatility, the questions must be asked: What is the past history of the stock? What is the likelihood of its making a change? and What would the percentage of that change be?

Hey . . . Notice the water is getting warmer? Hang on in there, dear reader. See, it's less and less deep the closer we come . . .

Puff . . . puff . . . just a few more feet. . . .

7

KNEE-DEEP

Yeah . . . PUFF . . . puff, just a few more feet. They say there is a broken heart for every light on Broadway and an ulcer for every formula on Wall Street.

Try to remember that in the real world an option's actual price is not necessarily the same as the one computed by a formula. As I have said, a majority of the pages in most serious options books are dedicated to the computation of what is formularized fair value (a futile exercise indeed). With the liquidity brought on by the listed options and the rapidity brought on by technology, and added to that the cost of commission, the small discrepancy that might exist momentarily between "fair" and actual value is generally not worth the effort and the fair-value question becomes a moot one. In any case one should not base a buying decision on the belief that such and such an option is underpriced, no more than one should choose one option over another simply because the premium is less or the time is more. An option, like life, is more intricate than that. It must all be worked out on a risk-reward basis.

Anyway, at first you will use a full-service broker who will explain the steps to you and shield you from beginner's errors. Start slowly. There are tricks to buying options, some elemental, some refined, some aggressive, some passive. There are shortcuts that simplify, and those that are fatal. If formulas turn out to be your thing, there are a zillion to choose from right off the rack or you can tailor-make your own. There are outright sins of omission and sins of convenience. You will grow to know them all, tricks and formulas, too. Gradually, you will learn to know what works best for you. Start slowly. Eventually, you will arrive at *your* risk-reward ratio (which is the real basis on which one must make a decision to purchase What When).

If the option is selling for more than the computed price, it is said to be overvalued, and undervalued if it is selling at a price less than the computed one. The delta of an option is another important consideration. The delta is often called the hedge ratio, and is usually expressed as a number between 0 and 1. The delta of an option is the theoretical amount by which the option will increase or decrease in price for a one-point move in the stock. However, delta is not a constant. Its value changes as the stock price changes. Your broker will have a delta model to assist you in the beginning with this complex mathematical formulation so that you can choose with his aid which striking price is most advantageous to purchase. If the broker or the data service does not incorporate the volatility or delta hedge ratio in its computation, a not uncommon shortcut, his raw research will be lacking in sophistication and all subsequent analysis flowing from him will be similarly flawed. With the ever-increasing competitiveness of the market one need not work with inferior analysis or inferior brokerage houses.

Could we just take a quickie review before we reach the shore? (Sure, I know, you have it all down pat, but for my sake, okay?)

CALLS

Here is an example from the horse's mouth, the AMEX's "A Guide to Listed Options." Someone feels that a certain stock is going to rise, so:

> The call buyer anticipates that in purchasing the call he can participate in an increase in the value of the underlying stock by investing a fraction of the cost of the stock, *obtaining greater leverage* on his investment. He also is *limiting his risk,* since the most he can lose if he purchases the call is the cost of the option.
>
> Example:
>
>> On Feb. 15, the common stock of Industrial Corp. is selling at $40 a share and an Oct. 40 call can be purchased for $500 ($5 per share). An investor, anticipating an increase in the price of the underlying stock, buys a call for $500.

On Apr. 15, the common stock is selling at $46 a share and the Oct. 40 call is selling at $850. The investor can now sell his call for $850, realizing a $350 profit, less transaction costs, a 70% rate of return on the original investments.

The following comparison will illustrate the leverage it is possible to achieve through the purchase of options:

	CALL	STOCK
Bought February 15	$500.	$4000.
Sold April 15	850.	4600.
Profit (disregarding transaction costs)	350.	600.
% Return (not annualized)	70%	15%

If the stock does not rise, the call buyer can lose no more than the $500 (and transaction costs) he paid for the Industrial Corp. Oct. 40 call. He risks losing his entire investment in a short period of time if his expectations on the stock prove wrong, but he may be able to minimize this risk by selling his option in the secondary market while the option still has remaining time value. In contrast, had he purchased the stock for $4,000, he stands to lose more than the $500 option premium in the event the stock decreases in price, although he has a chance of recouping his loss if he continues to hold the stock and it later appreciates in value.

. . . appreciates in value, get it? Which is better, to spend $4,000 for 100 shares of stock at forty bucks a share and make $600? 15 percent on your money? (Don't forget also the risk of the bottom dropping out of your stock and a substantial part of your hard-earned four grand going south.) Or is it better to buy one call option at a 5-point premium (which means, since one option controls a hundred shares of stock, 5 × 100) for \$500 and making \$350, a 70 percent return on your money? That is leverage at work, and with the *limited* risk of only the *\$500*. Okay, don't rush out and price the Rolls-Royce just yet; you are going to win some and lose some and the ready cash may come in handy. All your deals will not turn to gold, but there are a few techniques to help you maximize those that do, and we will get to that in a moment. In the meantime, maybe it wouldn't hurt to take a walk past the showroom and peek in.

PUTS

Let's go back to the horse's mouth again. Someone feels that a certain stock is going to fall, so:

> The put buyer anticipates that if the price of the underlying shares falls, he will earn a greater percentage return on invested funds than if he sold the stock "short," thus obtaining greater leverage on his investment. Like the call buyer, he also is *limiting his risk,* since the most he can lose is the cost of the option.
>
> Example:
>
>> On February 15, the common stock of Industrial Corp. is selling at \$50 a share and an Oct. 50 put is purchased for \$500 (\$5 per share).
>> On April 15, the common stock is selling at \$40 a share and the Oct. 50 put can be sold for \$1100, realizing a \$600 profit (less transaction costs).

	PUT	SOLD SHORT
Bought February 15	$500.	
Sold stock "short" Feb. 15 (50% required)		$2500.
Sold put April 15	$1100.	
Covered short April 15		$3500.
Profit (disregarding transaction costs)	$600.	$1000.
% Return (not annualized)	120%	40%

> If the stock does not fall, the put buyer can lose no more than the $500 premium plus transaction costs. This loss, however, represents 100% of his invested capital. Like the call buyer, the put holder might be able to minimize this loss by selling his option prior to expiration in the secondary market. His risk is substantially less than if he had sold the stock short, since the short seller's risk is only limited by the appreciation potential of the underlying shares.

Are you with me still? Intimidated, huh? Don't be. Understanding is to a large part a question of habit. Actually, it is no more complicated than boiling an egg. Boiling an egg, huh? Okay, skeptic, let's just for a moment do a brief exercise and pretend we are starting from scratch with an egg, as we have started from scratch with options. Look, try to imagine the instructions. Many of the considerations in egg-boiling are so automatic they are second nature and we don't even think of them.

First you must get a pot . . . Try and find a pot in which the amount of water can cover a large part of the egg . . . Okay, see what I mean? Of course, you would say, I understand that. Of course nothing! It's because you know it that it seems so natural! Forty-nine out of fifty of the things we do every day we are simply not aware of, because of how well we know the steps. Anyway, let's go on with our egg-boiling experiment . . . Find a stove, light the stove, and if it is gas and has no pilot light, use a match . . . Be careful to strike the match before you turn on the gas. Of course, of course, you say, you know that! Don't get mad . . . see what I mean? . . . even boiling an egg when starting from scratch seems like a complicated affair. That's my point! Soon this affair, options trading, will be second nature to you.

A call option is the right to buy. A put option is the right to sell. You could almost say that they're exactly the opposite. The most basic point of divergence is that when the underlying asset increases in price, the value of the call increases and the put decreases, and when the underlying asset drops, the put increases and the call decreases. Since most of the elements that apply to puts also pertain to calls, you will have a sneaky opportunity to review one as we contemplate the other. Puts and calls of the same underlying stock class have the same date of expiration and also the same striking price; if there is a 50's call, there will be a 50's put. Not too long ago, when many stocks had only call options, it was not necessary to designate call or put.

However, now you must say August 40 call or August 40 put.

When the stock price exceeds the striking price of a call, the call is said to be in-the-money. The amount by which the stock is in-the-money is called the intrinsic value. It is just the opposite for a put. When the striking price of a put is below the price of the stock, it is said to be in-the-money. If the stock price is below the striking price of a call, it is said to be out-of-the-money, and when the stock price is above the striking price of a put, the put is said to be out-of-the-money. For example, if a put has a strike price at 80 and the stock is selling at 87, the put is said to be 7 points out-of-the-money.

As the underlying stock goes down, the value of the put option increases and the value of the call option decreases. An interesting and sometimes useful characteristic of a put option is that an in-the-money put loses its time value premium more quickly than an in-the-money call does. Also, when the underlying stock and strike price of an option coincide, the call premium is usually more than the put premium.

The same four major factors shape the price of the call and the put option, and the same various minor influences are pushing and pulling: the treasury bill rate, the current interest rate, the dividend of the underlying stock, and here are a few more lesser determinants for consideration—market dynamics, market psychology, supply and demand.

If a price curve of a put option is developed, one discovers that it, just as for the call option, has a nonlinear rate of decay. Options lose their time premium more quickly as the expiration date nears. Also, the more volatile the underlying stock, the more costly the price of the option . . . risk-reward, tit for tat. The larger volatility leaves more risk for the seller and therefore he charges more. The higher volatility also leaves the potential for more reward for the buyer, so the buyer is willing to pay more.

Whereas the dividend of the underlying stock is a minus factor on the price of call options, it is a positive factor for put options. That's true because as stock goes ex-dividend it will be reduced by the amount of the dividend. The stock will decrease in price and therefore the put will be even more valuable. If a put buyer knows the stock is going to go ex-dividend, he is willing to pay a higher price.

In trading, like poker, it is crucial to know when to hold and when to fold. If, for example, you were sure stock XYZ (the name has been changed to protect the guilty) was going to rocket to the moon, but instead, heaven forbid, drops like a stone, or just sits there like a toad, you must have the mental toughness to liquidate your position and minimize your losses. If on the other hand, as you predicted, knock on wood, the stock should *zoom* in the case of a call or *plummet* in the case of a put, you should know at what point to take the money and run.

Most investors if they buy an option and it moves from 4, say, to 8, are willing to sell. On the other hand, if the premium had been lower, say 2, many find it more difficult to sell when the premium reaches 4. You mustn't think in how many points you made, but in the percentage on your investment. In both cases, the money has been doubled and therefore a gain of 100 percent has been made on the investment.

What the heck, let's blue-sky it for a moment and count our chickens before they hatch. Let's just say, no matter how you got there, be it through some clue in the price/earnings ratio, which is what you get when you divide the market price of a stock by its earnings per share; be it through insight obtained by studying the trader's index, which is what you get when you find the ratio of advancing stock issues to retreating issues and then factor in the ratio of advances and declines volumewise; be it a hunch gleaned from some old friend like delta, beta, annualization, or Harvey's big toe, let's just say for the sake of discussion, singularly or through a combination of ingredients, you have chosen right. What then?

Well, if you buy a call and the stock rises nicely, there are four scenarios for locking in the profit, two of which are simple and two of which are complicated.

1. Hold
2. Fold
3. Roll-up
4. Combination (synthetic bull spread)

ONE (simple) If you do nothing and the stock continues to rise, your profit grows larger. There is always the risk, however, that the stock may reverse itself, wiping out your gain.

TWO (simple) Liquidate the position by selling the call and taking the profit. No more risk but also no more potential for gain.

THREE (complicated) Sell the original call, pocket initial investment, and use the profit to buy whatever amount of new calls with a higher striking price (usually 5 to 10 points up) the remainder will allow—rolling up, as it is called. The buyer is now playing for free and cannot get hurt and yet is still in a position to make more profit.

FOUR (complicated) Invent a combination. The normal strategy is to create a bullish spread by selling out-of-the-money calls against the profitable call; but selling requires posting a margin. So what to do? What is almost equivalent to selling a call but avoids the added money . . . don't answer all at once. You got it! . . . buying a put. So that's what we do. The buyer cannot lose and can potentially have a limited reward.

Putwise, if the buyer's underlying stock goes down, the lucky investor can make follow-up moves reminiscent of those that the call buyer made when the stock rose.

1. He could sell a put and liquidate the position for profit.
2. He could do nothing and continue to hold the put.
3. He could sell his in-the-money put and pocket the original investment, then use the profits to purchase out-of-the-money puts.

4. He could hold on to the put and in the meantime buy a call.

. . . Terra firma, dry sand, we made it, well, just like they say, every voyage begins with that first step.

8

DIAMOND ON THE SAND

Having second thoughts . . . eh? Feeling sheepish because they say he is lost who hesitates? Never you mind, friend, prudence is not a sin in the trading game.

We have come quite a piece . . . What do you say we figure out the universe and simultaneously catch our breath here on the beach (blue sky overhead, yonder swaying palms, warm sand underneath)?

Risk, reward, struggle, ambition . . . I daresay the world hasn't changed that much, not more than an iota or two since we've been away. And you, dear reader, fortitude, tenacity, intelligence still intact? Well, the map says your reward, the options treasure chest chock-full of rubies and pearls, is still up there buried somewhere beyond the beach, just waiting. Look at it like this: Wealth is closer than it used to be and poverty is still the pits. Risk involves not only the money and the courage to plunk down your pennies. Oh no, would that it were that cut-and-dry, that simple. Risk means concentrating, the sweat-equity of learning, and toughest of all, enduring the agony of discombobulation and confusion.

On the subject of confusion, not just in options, but in life . . . people often wonder, "If I have chosen the correct path, why don't I feel perfectly, 100 percent right about it?" Well, where does the other side of a choice go when a decision is made? It doesn't disappear, and unless you acknowledge that the merits on the unchosen side still remain, they will confuse and nag at you. Remember, a decision is a balancing act. You add up the pros and cons on both sides, make a decision, and move on. If there weren't merits on the other side, it wouldn't have been a hard decision in the first place. What the heck, life is ambiguity—like watching your mother-in-law drive off a cliff in your brand-new Cadillac.

There is an old proverb, probably Chinese, that says if a decision has 55 percent in its favor, count that as a lucky day; if it has 65 percent going for it, you have been truly blessed; and if there is more than 70 percent on your side, forget it, for you're lying to yourself, or dead and gone to heaven.

Tired? Yes, I know it does seem unfair, but the truth is, no matter how hard it is to earn it, you will also have to struggle to keep it, at first anyway. Luckily, like everything else, there is a knack to making your money make money, and you will soon catch on. Nevertheless, the road to riches isn't that easy; if it were, there would be far more traffic on it. Press on, be of stout heart . . . What have you got to lose anyway? Your buying power is being eroded more each day. A penny saved will soon be a penny lost. You will have to run just to stand still.

Are the various and sundry options theories confusing you? Well, they did that to me, too. The truth is that the theories themselves are often confused. (A theory is how some people characterize something that they know for an absolute certainty—maybe—yet want to leave themselves an exit, just in case.) Most theories, options included, suffer from simultaneous overreach and tunnel vision. That, of course, is because we human beings have this pompous need to explain everything, even that which we don't fully understand. On the one hand, that's the arrogant nature of the beast called man, but on the other hand, you can't knock it too much for pomposity is a by-product of the same motor that has pushed, pulled, and driven us from scratching for berries, termites, and lion leftovers on some savannah to dining on filet mignon. (A recent hypothesis advanced by Robert Blumenshine, of the University of California at Berkeley, *Science News*, vol. 127, no. 10, has our ancestors not the romantic hunters of idealized dreams but scavengers with a modus operandi closer to a hyena's than a cheetah's.) I doubt whether a creature a few million years ago if offered the choice, say, of a nice sharp tusk growing out of his forehead or having a few additional grams of some gray matter stuffed into his skull would have chosen the latter. Can't you just imagine some early guy grumbling bitterly about his larger brain and how he had been genetically shortchanged, not realizing that his capacity to realize would be his key to achieving the pinnacle of creation, not realizing that it would give him the ambition and ability to improve himself. Here we are back at a better life, back at options once again.

Sure the world is in turmoil and growing more so every day.

> The fabric of civilization today is woven of millions of threads. No spot in it is so strong that it will not feel some effect from a weakening at any point. Are the people of India suffering depression? Then Lancashire cotton mills must curtail operation, American cotton farmers sell their crop at low prices, fertilizer manufacturers suffer in consequence. A bumper wheat crop in the Argentine may have similar repercussions all around the world. In an obscure corner of the Balkans, as the world discovered in 1914, the act of an assassin may wipe out currencies, destroy some industries and create others thousands of miles away, open new trade routes and close many old ones, upset the whole balance of international payments, create new standards of land values in the wheat fields of Kansas.
>
> **Philip L. Carret,**
> *The Tides of Speculation,* 1930

That observation was made more than fifty years ago. Through ever-increasing interconnectedness we are shrinking into the global village Marshall McLuhan predicted twenty years ago. Events ricochet off one another with dizzying speed, OPEC games begetting gunfights at filling station pumps in New Jersey, acid rain begetting dead fish, Bhopal begetting methyl isocyanate, on and on. If it ain't Bubonic Plague, it's AIDS. The overview has always been pretty much a mess, and the long view is you're dead. Now scientists, with the aid of iridium tests, claim that our solar system is a binary one, and that every 26 or 27 million years our sun's fraternal sister, aptly dubbed Nemesis, makes a pass in the vicinity of Earth and wipes the slate clean with a mass extinction (like what happened with the dinosaurs). Past, present, future . . . turmoil everywhere you look . . . a birth certificate is nothing but a death certificate anyway. In the meantime, back at the ranch, how about that Rolls-Royce, or steak with candles on the table, and controlling the destiny you *do* have left?

One of the most prized characteristics of a stock is its volatility, and turmoil is nothing but volatility in work clothes. Since volatility is opportunity, it follows that turmoil is nothing but opportunity in dungarees.

You must apply yourself religiously, yet the quest for wealth, through options, or through anything else for that matter, should not be allowed to become a religion, a crucial distinction and one you must never forget. To paraphrase the Bible, what does it matter if you gain the world and lose your soul in the process? The tone of this book is in part a talisman, an attempt to ward off the wicked spells of the Moolahnites who choose to rule by sorcery and fright. I believe in options as Napoleon believed in warfare, that the psychology is three times more important than the equipment!

If being bombarded with dubious theories and models masquerading as immutable realities, "price discovery," et al, bothers you; if the routine necessity of having to actually manipulate and employ semi-bogus strategies and formulas, each having the impunity to claim sovereignty over the truth, troubles you; if the juggling of nebulous numbers is more than you can take; if it creates within you unbearable distress, then so long and adios. I have arranged through special dispensation to get you back home without your having to endure the arduous return journey. It's easy. Simply say, "I renounce success," click your heels three times, close this book, and be free of it all.

Oh, so you're going to stay? Good, then just let's lie here a few moments longer, watching the clouds move slowly in the sky, and try to pinpoint your position in the financial community. I guess your title (nothing like a title to locate oneself) would be potential speculator/trader in the art of options gambling, or student-speculator/trader of the Options Game. A speculator differs from an investor in proportion to the speed with which he tries to accumulate money and avoid risk. An investor prefers to accumulate money much more slowly in exchange for taking less risk. However, with the constantly accelerating rate of dollar erosion, investing can be illusory. Your capital can actually deteriorate faster than it can be replenished by the low rate of return from many secure investments. General Douglas MacArthur once said, "There is no security, only opportunity."

At any rate, the Options Game being as fast and as daring as it is, we are speculators, not investors.

Stripped of the mumbo jumbo, a speculator's business is to spot cracks, inconsistencies, and potential inconsistencies in the universe and then to convert the imbalances created by such deviations into moneymaking opportunities. Easier said than done. To spot that something is out of kilter, one has to keep a steady keel oneself. That is what the majority of models and formulas and theories are about: steadying the keel, finding out if the keel is off-center, if so, by how much, if not, when will it be and at what price? That's all supply and demand is really saying, or, more accurately, asking. In short, which way is the market going?

There are a couple of speculator/trader occupational hazards you should be warned about.

1. The quest for the ultimate equation to steady the keel (a perennial Moolahnite fantasy) has spawned a cult of numbers. Granted, numbers can be an effective tool.

> In my view every economic fact, whether or not it is of such a nature as to be expressed in numbers, stands in relation as cause and effect to many other facts: and since it never happens that all of them can be expressed in numbers, the application of exact mathematical methods to those which can is nearly always a waste of time, while in the large minority of cases it is positively misleading; and the world would have been further on its way forward if the work had never been done at all.
>
> **Alfred Marshall,**
> Letter to A. I. Bowley, March 3, 1901

But there has been quite a bit of water under the bridge since Marshall wrote Bowley (these days the poor man is surely spinning in his grave) and numbers have been elevated to a miracle-working status, one that would make a snake-oil salesman blush. What is the great attraction of numbers? Well, they seem so uncorruptible, so official, so carved in stone. In actuality numbers are subservient. They can be lied about, lied to and twisted, and they take abuse without complaint.

> To tell us that every species of thing is endowed with an occult specific quality by which it acts and produces manifest effects, is to tell us nothing; but to derive two or three general principles of motion from phenomena, and afterwards to tell us how the properties and actions of all corporeal things follow from those manifest principles, would be a very great step.
>
> **Isaac Newton,**
> *Opticks,* 1704

From time to time some shyster number-manipulating market analyst will shout "Eureka!" and proclaim that he understands the properties and actions of all corporeal things, but so far, the which-way-goes-the-market question remains unsolved.

It is doubtful, in this higgledy-piggledy world jiggling at a zillion times per second, with hundreds of variables per equation, that anyone knows the horizontal of everything, and so the speculator has to specialize in order to cope.

Some things, numbers and specialization included, seem to have a predilection for growing out of control (it can be a short hop from logic to travesty). And that brings us to occupational hazard number two.

2. Specialization touches a vulnerable spot in the ego chain. There are two life forces battling inside of everyone. One says, go out and find adventure, conquer the universe, achieve. The other is saying, stay here in the back of the cave where it's safe. The factions of the mind battle back and forth in healthy competition from the cradle to the grave. Specialization can disrupt this delicate balance. Specialization requires one to shrink one's focus and concentrate heavily on a particular niche, and that niche can soon seem to be all of life. If one is not careful (especially if one is hardworking and successful), the mind, fatigued and desperate for relief of any kind, brainwashes itself and reaches an ingenious solution to the Conqueror versus Safe Struggle. The resolution is always the same. The brain declares that the niche is *all* there is to life. That way it satisfies both forces. The safe-cave side is satisfied because the mind reigns supreme in the universe of the niche and therefore has nothing to fear and the adventurer/conqueror is satisfied for having conquered the entire world. The niche is not the entire world, of course. That is the illusion. This self-deception is not the monopoly of Wall Street. This "my-niche-is-the-whole-universe" syndrome is rampant wherever there is insularity, intensity, and success, and not surprisingly Wall Street leads the pack with the highest proportion per capita of these exalted personages.

Whether you avoid becoming a numbers freak and/or a vainglorious Moolahnite is up to you.

And now to the Big Enigma. If the fundamentalists are right, why are there millionaire technicians? If the technicians are right, why are there fundamentalists making millions? What about the Market-Timing boys, the Random Walkers, the Contrarians, and all the sects in between who are making their bundles? How do they fit in?

Take the two major sects, the technicians and the fundamentalists. The technicians believe that all the known information about a company is automatically reflected in the price and that the market works perfectly, while the fundamentalists think that the market is often out of alignment, and that by calculating discrepancies from basic information they can determine whether to sell or buy. Each champions his own method fiercely. Surely one must be a liar, or at best a charlatan. Which one is right? In actuality, neither.

The secret to good teaching is to get in touch with the inner core of the pupil, a core each human being carries within himself. That core is the will to be *more*. Take championship fighters, for instance—some are sluggers, some are skillful boxers. Each believes his road is the right one. It probably is the right road for him, but it does not follow, therefore, that a different style is wrong. If the fighter's style allows him to get in touch with his core and come out for the bell, if it gives him the strength to struggle up from the canvas, then Amen. Where we often go astray is in believing that there is only one way. In fact, the way itself is almost incidental except as it contributes to the primary mission of allowing us to get in touch with our core. Step back from the chaos and hurly-burly, and what do you see?

I see a line threading through the lives of successful people. I detect a common denominator, one that has led me to believe that the championship fighter's technique is only a minority shareholder in his success. I believe that, more important than style, formula, technique, or strategy, a person who is a champion in any endeavor has managed to tap his inner potential.

I would like to suppose that when someone extols one school of options trading over another, or what have you, the extoller may be guilty of tunnel vision, but it is an effort often made in good faith by a person who does not realize that what works for him may not work for the world. In essence the person is trying to pass on to others that which allowed him to get in touch with himself. Unaware of their true potential, people usually overemphasize the method. Seldom does a person realize that the method that triggered him or her is only a small part of what caused their success. The method is only the catalyst, not the core. You are the core.

Faith in a method, style, or technique, as comforting as that faith might be, is not the secret to success. The secret lies in the diamond within your breast. Whichever method harnesses that awesome power is your key to success. I do not use the word *awesome* lightly. That diamond in your breast is what has pulled man up from and out of many a mess (yes, got him into his share of messes, too). What are you? What do I see resting on the sand? I see a diamond in the rough, encased in the form of man.

Whichever method most closely corresponds to your perspective, activates your core, and allows you to marshal your forces most efficiently is you, your guiding power. Trust yourself. . . .

> By depending on expertise, we have become less dependent on ourselves. By so downgrading our trust in our intuitions and feelings, we settle too often for the false comforts of doctrines and beliefs. Considering the predictive records of economists and other information specialists, it is quite clear that such trust has too often been unrewarded. In effect, by attempting to fit life's events into the framework of rigid form, we tend to exhaust our energies by trying to freeze the flow of the current.
>
> **Bennett W. Goodspeed,**
> *The Tao Jones Average*

Don't think of pressure as your enemy. After all, what turns a plain ole lump of coal into a diamond anyway? . . . Yessireee, Pressure! Used correctly, pressure can be exhilarating. Besides, it gets the adrenaline racing and keeps you regular to boot. (It's true, pressure is a great laxative. A little tension, a little fright can work wonders, right? Everyone has heard the expression "scared unto a call of nature.")

We are going to take it slow, so think about the method that might suit you. Don't rush yourself, and in case you don't find what turns you on, use the bibliography provided at the end of the journey. (In fact, even if you do find the method that suits you, use the bibliography.)

Life is pretty much like a balloon. What I mean is you get out what you put in . . . speaking of that, break's over.

BOOK II

THE TREK

9

BLAST-OFF

Resting on one's laurels and philosophizing are nice but . . .

> *"We got a piece to go before we pitch camp . . ."*
> **Mule skinner**
>
> *"Let us then be up and doing . . ."*
> **Poet**
>
> *"Move it or lose it . . ."*
> **Drill sergeant**

Don't be fooled. The investment trail just ahead at the edge of the sand, sloping and winding upward as it disappears into the palms, is not a path for the dilettante. You must pay constant attention to each step. A few wrong turns and you can end up in bankruptcy instead of Shangri-la. Investing is a two-way street. You can win and you can lose. Approach each new area, bend, clearing, and water hole carefully, like a porcupine making love.

MOVE I. THINKING AND PLANNING

Think about and decide how much you can afford to speculate. Only you can decide. First, calculate your income. Now deduct your expenditures and you'll arrive at a fixed amount that you must be willing to risk.

Next, decide on a method and schedule of disbursement: whether you want to invest on a monthly, quarterly, or biannual schedule. Will it come from savings or a second job? If you're thinking of throwing caution to the wind and plopping down a large sum all at once, don't! Start slowly. Imagine every trade on paper first to get a feel for the market. Here is how you do it. Pick an option in your mind and pretend you bought it and follow it through just as if you had.

When you actually begin trading, an ultraconservative approach is to place 90 percent of your after-expense resources into money market or CD funds and invest the remaining 10 percent in options. Under no circumstances should you buy more than five contracts the first time.

Does your approach consider the long overview, or are you more concerned about quick capital gains for the short term? It's important that your method and approach toward risk-taking in options be reviewed within the context of not only how much money you have available but how much time and also how much psychic energy you have to spend. Be sure your life-style and psychological temperament are compatible with the scope of the venture, especially at the beginning; otherwise, you may wind up biting off more than you can chew.

In the beginning, you are bound to make some mistakes. The important thing is to try to avoid those that can put you out of the game. One of those costly mistakes is inflexibility. When you see the market is going against you in a big way, it's usually better to get out of the game with half a loaf than no loaf at all.

As you develop your trading plan, make sure money to meet monthly bills and emergency family needs has been accounted for and set aside. This would include insurance for health and property as well as the educational needs of the family.

Know and understand that the capital that you are now putting into options is risk capital; that is, capital that you are willing to risk losing in order that you may benefit if your bet pays off.

If you're on the way up in your job, and your salary is increasing, you might want to risk a little more than if you were on a fixed income. If you're at a stage where kids are out of the house, you may want to invest in options in conjunction with an IRA or pension plan. If you are in business for yourself, you may want to include options in your portfolio as a way of financing potential growth or annual bonuses. Employee investing in options may also be a way to develop team spirit.

MOVE II. BUDGETING YOUR CAPITAL

Sit down and write out a budget, which should look something like the following.

BUDGET

ANNUAL INCOME

My annual income	________________
Spouse's annual income	________________
Other income	________________
TOTAL INCOME	________________

ANNUAL EXPENSES

Mortgage or rent	________________
Insurance	________________
Taxes	________________
Vacation	________________
Loan repayments	________________
Living expenses	________________
Education	________________
Rainy-day fund	________________
TOTAL EXPENSES	________________

Now subtract total expenses from total income to arrive at the amount of capital you will be able to risk.

RISK CAPITAL ________________

Undercapitalization can be a serious problem. A major reason many businesses or investment programs fail is that they are undercapitalized. If you find you do not have as much as you would like in the risk capital column, you may want to reduce the amount of some frill in your expenses category or cut back on the ambitiousness of your investment program.

MOVE III. SETTING A DATE

Decide when you want to begin. Write the date down on the calendar and make an appointment with yourself. Also remember you will want to have in cash whatever your risk capital dollar figure is. This is a cash-buying investment plan. Consider your schedule. When will the funds be available? Most important, don't procrastinate. Set a date to do it and stick to it.

MOVE IV. CHOOSING A BROKER

Now we need to locate a friendly native guide. You will want to shop around when you pick your broker. Take a close look at advertisements listed in *The Wall Street Journal*, *Barron's*, and other financial publications. Also, your local library will most likely have books in the reference department of the business section naming brokerage firms with their financial ranking and customer account volume. These resources will make you aware of the different names of the companies as well as familiarize you with some of the financial language that you will be coming in contact with.

A FULL-SERVICE BROKER

Starting off, you will probably be best served by a full-service broker. A full-service broker is just what the name implies, a broker who will advise and counsel you on strategy as well as provide you with research materials concerning both your trading strategy and the options contract you choose to trade. It will be helpful if the broker you choose within the firm has had experience with options trading. Larger firms will most likely have authorities who concentrate specifically on options contracts. In addition, the opportunity of talking back and forth about your strategy and trades with a full-service broker will further familiarize you with the terms and workings of the markets.

THE DISCOUNT BROKER

A discount broker is different from a full-service broker in that the discount broker offers only minimal advice and does not aid you with even the basic trading strategies such as fundamental or technical analysis, or instruct you in the use of charts, graphs, or give you the benefit of his experience. Therefore, the customer is truly on his own. True enough, the discount broker offers prices maybe as much as 50 percent lower than a traditional full-service broker, but the assistance you get will also be less. The primary concern of the discount broker is only to execute the customer's order as quickly and efficiently as possible.

An intermediate broker? With Wall Street, who knows?

Change being the password. For instance, Wall Street's largest discount brokerage organization has grown from two crummy rooms in San Francisco on "May Day" (as it is now called by Moolahnites, the deregulation of brokerage commissions having taken place on May 1, 1975) into the largest discount brokerage house, with ninety-two branches, a million customers, half a million active accounts, and about 20 percent of the discount business, totaling a revenue of $148 million in 1984. In their efforts to attract large institutions they are offering limited research information and seem to be in the process of creating a new intermediate animal known as a "full-service discount broker," in the meantime sweetening the pie for the small investor by implementing buy and sell capabilities via home and office computer links.

PROS, CONS, AND NOTWITHSTANDINGS

Nevertheless, whether you choose a full-service or a discount broker, there are factors you should be aware of, for instance . . .

Is your agreement in writing, and does it have any special clauses you may not agree with?

Is the firm a financially stable outfit? Does it make its year-end financial statements public? Does the firm manage other money accounts in such a way as to present a conflict of interest to your financial objectives?

Does the firm employ brokers sufficiently knowledgeable in the area of options?

In the case of a discount broker, is the discount based

on volume of trading or is it independent of volume? Do you have to maintain a certain balance to receive the discounted rate?

When you want funds, will your broker promptly mail or wire them to you? Will you receive accounting statements promptly?

Are there any minimum commission fees? Are there any hidden costs reflected in your purchase and sales report?

If you are unsure as to what your position is, can you call in to get an update on where you stand?

Does the firm handle its margin policy in a responsible way? When margins are adjusted (raised or lowered) or when the options contract changes in some way, will your broker let you know promptly?

If there is a mistake on your trading account, can and will the firm expedite the necessary paperwork to correct it quickly?

On occasion a broker may execute your trade incorrectly, at which point you will of course refuse the trade. However, in order to minimize any mix-ups, it pays to record your telephone conversations with your broker when giving orders (on a cassette tape recorder). Most of the firms doing customer business on a regular basis tape-record all conversations as a way of protecting themselves against litigation claims which may be made against them relating to wrong orders.

How can a discount broker afford to compete? Mainly by incurring fewer expenses because he renders less service. A discount broker earns money from the commissions that the customer pays, but in the meantime, just like his full-service cousin, he earns interest from any excess cash lying dormant in the margin accounts. This interest is called the *float*.

In summary, you get what you pay for. With a full-service broker you will have the luxury of learning through research material and conversation, but you will pay for counseling and services as part of your commissions. With a discount broker, on the other hand, you save on commissions but will have to put in the time and energy to do all of the necessary research as well as forgo the benefit of experience.

MOVE V. MAKING CONTACT

PHONE CONTACT

OK now, get a pencil and pad. Call a few brokers by phone and take notes. Ask the broker exactly what his office does. Make sure you are speaking with an actual broker. This is very important, because many of the people working in a brokerage firm, especially those who might be answering the phones, may have little or no understanding of the questions you will need to have answered. You will be amazed to see how much you can learn about the various firms and about the business just by using this method. Set up an appointment.

Don't open an account with a broker you've never seen, unless you know the firm by reputation, even if the broker promises you the lowest commission schedule you've ever heard. A fly-by-night broker can put you on a wrong track that will leave a bad taste in your mouth for years to come. Remember, sometimes cheap can turn out being very expensive.

FACE-TO-FACE

Realize that you have a choice. You may want to go with the largest established firm, Merrill Lynch, which has 445 domestic and 65 foreign offices with 4.8 million customer accounts, or you may want to try a medium-size broker with a few offices and with 5,000 to 10,000 customer accounts, or even a small broker with only one office and a couple of hundred customer accounts and is ranked near the bottom of the nearly two hundred brokerage firms operating in the U.S. of A.

The advantage of the big companies is that you may have a wider range of sophisticated research material available to you while the advantage of the small companies may be the offering of more personal attention from a broker who might have more time for your account.

Ask questions until you are satisfied with the answers. Remember, as the potential customer you have the power.

Don't let a broker bully you into submission with high sales technique and terminology you do not understand. Make them explain in clear language. And if they ask how much you plan to trade, don't name figures. Sidestep the question by saying something obtuse like you were referred to the firm by a close relative of the company's vice-president and that you plan to trade a sizable amount if you can get the right answers to your questions. You won't have to worry about them checking you out because many firms have a slew of vice-presidents.

Finally, ask the broker for an application to open an options trading account.

MOVE VI. OPENING AN ACCOUNT

Don't sign anything at the first interview. Take the account application home and study it. Go over the form slowly, at your leisure. Your options accounts application will list some of the following questions.

1. Investment goals (short-term, long-term)
2. Employment status
3. Marital status, number of dependents
4. Estimated net worth
5. Estimated liquid net worth
6. Annual income
7. Age

If you already have a regular equity account at a firm and you continue to use the firm, your statement may have to be reviewed before allowing you to open an options account.

Also be aware that there are different kinds of accounts:

Type 1. Only you as a customer can trade.

Type 2. As an investor you may open a discretionary account, meaning your broker trades your account based on what he thinks the market will do. This can be dangerous. *I do not recommend* this type of account.

Type 3. Third-party or fiduciary account, wherein someone other than the principal customer, such as your spouse or, in the case of an account opened in the name of the investment club, the treasurer, trades the account.

In addition, the material given to you

1. should not promise specific performance or make exaggerated or unreasonable claims.
2. should not contain false, confusing, or ambiguous language and should not make misleading statements.
3. should not imply that options trading is well suited for everyone.
4. in the case of conventional options should not claim that secondary markets will always exist.
5. should not only feature the rewards of options, omitting the risks.
6. should comply with the Securities Act of 1933 for prospectus delivery dates.

The handling of your customer account is mandated under Rule 405 of the Securities Act of 1933 as follows:

RULE 405
Diligence as to Accounts
Every member organization is required through a general partner, a principal executive officer or a person or persons designated under the provisions of Rule 342(b) (1) (2342) to (1) use diligence to learn the essential facts relative to every customer, every order, every cash or margin account accepted or carried by such organization and every person holding power of attorney over any

> account accepted or carried by such organization.
> Supervision of Accounts
> (2) Supervise diligently all accounts handled by registered representatives of the organization.
> Approval of Accounts
> (3) Specifically approve the opening of an account prior to or promptly after the completion of any transaction for the account of or with a customer . . .

Remember, your broker's job is to give you the best advice possible. He cannot guarantee you against a loss nor share in the profits or losses of your account. However, his consultation can prove invaluable in interpreting market trends and research data, especially at the beginning.

Now let's rustle up our friendly full-service native guide and head inland.

10

STEPPING INTO THE SYSTEM

The brokerage firm should be the cornerstone of your research information. Your broker should be able to immediately quote you the prices on any listed option that you find interesting. He should act as the executor of your order as well as your guide. Many of the brokerage companies have newsletters which are available usually for free or on a subscription basis. Trade publications can be very helpful to you in the growing process. Foremost among these are *The Wall Street Journal* (daily newspaper), *Barron's* (weekly newspaper), *Futures* (monthly magazine), and *Business Week* (weekly magazine). They often talk about the pros and cons of various stocks, options, and commodities. In addition, some will include market projections by traders, economists, and analysts.

Such publications will keep you up-to-date on the world of high finance, as they frequently feature interesting articles on options. In fact, you may want to make trade publications a permanent part of your financial library.

Uncle Sam is one of the biggest, least expensive, and most accurate sources of financial information. Each public company must file a 10K report annually with the Securities and Exchange Commission. These reports are likely to include harder information not highlighted in the regular annual reports designed more for glamorized public consumption and stockholders' meetings. You can obtain a copy of a company's 10K report by writing the SEC in Washington, D.C.

Don't be discouraged if at first some of the concepts and nomenclature pass you by. You will be amazed at how rapidly you become familiar with the various terms and their applications. Taking a step in that direction, let's look at the following terms. Some you will have seen before and some will be new. I have chosen to present them in order of their appearance, as they say in the movies; in other words, the order in which you might encounter them as you proceed step by step in selecting an option to trade.

TERMS

OPTIONS CONTRACT

What kind of contract are you buying? Is it based on stocks, commodities, indexes, or futures? Is the option itself considered an equity or a commodity? Is the option in- or out-of-the-money? How liquid is the contract? What are the exercise prices and expiration dates?

OPTIONS EXCHANGE

The physical location where options are traded: Chicago Board of Trade, American Stock Exchange, Philadelphia Stock Exchange, New York Stock Exchange, Pacific Stock Exchange.

EXERCISE PRICE

The price per share (or other unit) at which the holder of an option can buy and/or sell the underlying security. The exercise price is also referred to as the striking price. If Mr. A buys 2 July 40 calls for $8, the exercise price is 40.

EXPIRATION DATE

The latest time at which an options contract may be exercised (also known as maturity date). Until the summer of 1985, all CBOE options had a standardized expiration date set at three-month intervals. Since that time the exchanges have been experimenting with pilot programs testing the viability of monthly expiration. The longest term of an option does not exceed nine months (as opposed to thirteen months in the case of over-the-counter options). The three cycles are (1) January, April, July, October, (2) February, May, August, November, and (3) March, June, September, December. All options expire at 5:00 P.M. Eastern time on the Saturday following the third Friday of the specified month. For example, Oct 1986 options would expire at 5:00 P.M. on Saturday October 24, 1986. *Note:* Near expiration date an option becomes less valuable due to loss of time value.

IN-THE-MONEY

An option is said to be in-the-money when, in the case of the call, the strike price is below the market price (strike price 40, market price 50) and, in the case of a put, the strike price is above the market price of the underlying security. In-the-money options are the most expensive.

INTRINSIC VALUE

The amount by which a call or put option is in-the-money. In other words, it is the difference between the striking price and market price. If market price of the underlying asset were trading at 40, an April 30 call would reflect 10 points intrinsic value.

OUT-OF-THE-MONEY

An option is said to be out-of-the-money when the strike price is *above* market price in the case of a *call* (strike is 60, market at 52) or in the case of a *put,* the strike price is *below* the market price (strike price 52, market price 60). Out-of-the-money options are the least expensive.

OPEN INTEREST

The number of outstanding options contracts which have been issued by the exchange. Each time a new contract is made between a buyer and a seller, the open interest is increased by one. The most liquid contracts are usually the ones with the highest open-interest figure.

After all of the aforementioned factors have been considered and a choice has been made, the next step is to inquire about the options price. Don't get too rigid. This is Moolahnite territory. Stay flexible. For example, a premium's cost can be the beginning as well as the end. Perhaps the entire sequence happened in reverse, starting, say, when you noticed or it was pointed out to you that a premium was cheap.

PREMIUM

The price you pay for your option is called its premium. That price reflects four factors:

1. *The price of the underlying stock or commodity.* If the price of the underlying asset is rising in value, the price of the call option is also rising, but the put value is diminishing.
2. *Volatility.* Volatility is the degree of fluctuation in the price of the underlying asset, the theory being that the more the price fluctuates, the more chances the option has of winning; therefore, the higher the expected volatility of the underlying asset, the higher the price of the option.
3. *Time value.* As the option nears expiration, the amount of time it has to become valuable diminishes; therefore, the nearer the expiration date of an option, the less time value will be reflected in its price.
4. *Striking price.* If the option is in-the-money, it will cost more than if it is out-of-the-money.

The following terms are not absolutely necessary for you to know in order to trade but are included because they are excellent checkpoints. Familiarity with them as they are bantered about will make your trading an immediately pleasurable experience, and that's not a bad reason in itself.

THE BUYER
You, the purchaser of a put or call option.

THE GUARANTOR
Who guarantees your payoff should you buy an option and it becomes more valuable? If it's a listed option, the guarantor is the OCC (Options Clearing Corporation), a nonprofit organization that conducts the accounting business of option trades between exchange members as well as supervises margin requirements and issues exercise notices. Remember, when you buy an option, your agreement is really with the OCC acting as an escrow agent for both sides.

WRITER
The seller or grantor of a put or call option. The options writer takes a premium for the buyer but is at unlimited risk if the market should go against him. To ensure that payment will be made, the OCC requires the writer to put up monies known as margin as insurance against default.

MARGIN CALL
A demand from a brokerage firm to a customer for the deposit of additional cash (or securities). Suppose an

options writer sold you an Oct 30 call when the market was trading at 40, and suddenly the market went to 60. The OCC would require the call writer to put up the additional monies of 20 that would mark the difference between his original margin, which would have been 30 percent of the stock value plus 10 in-the-money, and the present 30 points in-the-money.

LONG
To buy a stock or option before selling translates to being long the stock or option. Mary buys 3 Oct 20 calls, when before she had no Oct 20 calls. She is long 3 Oct 20 calls.

SHORT
To sell before buying in hopes of buying back later at a lower price.

DISCRETIONARY ACCOUNT
A customer account in which an officer, partner, or employee of a firm has been given the authority by the customer to buy and/or sell securities without prior consultation with or specific instruction from the customer. (As stated before, *dangerous*.)

LEVERAGE
The return potential per investment dollar; that is, any financial arrangement that increases the percentage return (or loss) from an investment.

OPENING BUY TRANSACTION
For the options buyer a transaction that establishes or increases a long position.

OPENING SELL TRANSACTION
For the options seller a transaction that establishes or increases a short position.

CLOSING SALE TRANSACTION
A transaction that reduces or eliminates a long position. When Mr. G first buys a call and later sells it, the sale is a closing sale transaction.

BULLISH
A belief that the market is going to rise.

BEARISH
A belief that the market is going to fall.

ORDERS

There is a special precise jargon your broker will use to convey his wishes to his counterpart on the exchange floor. This language is very specific in its instruction. Here are some orders you should be familiar with and what they do.

MARKET ORDER
A market order is an order to buy or sell immediately at the best obtainable price that the market will bear.

AT-THE-CLOSE ORDER
An at-the-close order is to be executed as near the closing of the day's trading session as practical.

AT-THE-OPENING ORDER

An at-the-opening order is to be executed at the beginning of the day's trading session, at a specific price or better or at the market.

DAY ORDER

A day order is an order to buy or sell, which if not executed expires at the end of the trading day on which it is entered.

A GTC (GOOD-TILL-CANCELED) ORDER

This is an order to buy or sell which remains in effect until it is either executed or canceled.

LIMIT ORDER

This is a specific price given by a customer above or below which the broker is not authorized to buy or sell. Mr. A will enter a limit order to buy at 50, because he is not willing to pay more than 50; *less* than 50, yes, but not more.

FILL OR KILL

This is a limit order which is to be executed in its entirety as soon as it is represented in the trading arena. If, however, it is not executed immediately, it is to be canceled. For example, on an order to buy 10 options for 12, Fill or Kill would demand that if the entire 10 options could not be purchased for 12 or better immediately, the floor trader must simply cancel the order.

TIME ORDER

This is an order which becomes a market or limit order at the specified time.

SPREAD ORDER

This is an order to buy one or more options contracts and to sell one or more options contracts at a specified differential in a different series of the same class of options. For example, sell 5 July 30 calls and buy 5 Oct 30 calls. The execution of spread orders is to be done simultaneously in order to attain the desired effect.

STOP ORDER TO BUY OR SELL

A stop order to buy becomes a market order when a transaction in the stock occurs at or above the stop price after the order is represented in the trading arena. A stop order to sell becomes a market order when a transaction in the stock occurs at or below the stop price. For example, if you were to buy a stock at 40 hoping the stock goes to 50, but in fact the stock starts moving downward, you might decide that if and when the stock hits, say, 32 you will want to bail out and limit your losses. You would place a stop loss order to sell at 32 . . . so why is it mentioned when the focus of the strategy is to buy only puts and calls, you might be asking? . . . a logical question . . . because loss orders aren't allowed in options, but as you become a more sophisticated options trader you might use options in connection with a stock-buying strategy.

On the floor of the exchange, where all of the order activities are carried out, each trader or floor broker quotes a bid (the price at which he is willing to buy) and an offer (the price at which he is willing to sell). The keeping of one's word on price quotes among traders is observed as a code of honor. Violation of that code will result in a trader being ostracized, on the basis that he's untrustworthy. For example: A trader shouts out to the trading arena that he wishes to buy 20 options for a price of 21, and another trader yells in response, "*Sold* at 21." If at the end of the day the market has gone against the buyer and he trys to deny knowledge of the trade or change the price intentionally, the word about his shenanigans will spread like wildfire among the other traders.

Honest mistakes are made, but a system of checks and balances exists to minimize them.

If you feel that you have gotten a bad execution as a customer, you can request a time and sales readout from the exchange. These computerized documents are recorded by clerks acting as monitors, employed by the exchange. As a customer it is important to know that you have the right to see this documented record. Oftentimes when customers get bad executions they simply shrug their shoulders and walk away. But that isn't your only recourse. Recently, customer protection has been addressed not only by the government but by private lawyers as well. In the back of *Barron's*, for example, there are attorneys who advertise that they will help recover investment losses.

One way to avoid major problems, especially when you are in the earlier stages of options buying, is to go with a reputable full-service broker who can offer an overall support system that will provide you not only with a data base for resource materials in the form of newsletters, charts, fundamental analysis, and interpretation of current market activity but also guidance into the world of options. Of course, as you gain expertise, you may develop your own charts, trends, and other tools and feel you can no longer benefit from using a full-service broker.

Let's pretend you are placing your order with a discount broker. You want to be the buyer of 2 XYZ calls which will expire in July and you want to buy at the strike price of 50 and at the çost of $3 per option. Your order to your broker should go as follows.

Buy 2 XYZ Jul 50 calls at 3.

Your broker will then phone in your trade to the exchange floor to be executed.

What if the broker tells you that the market is trading quickly and the price on the July 50s are selling at 4 and not 3, but that the April 50s are selling at 3. How would you tell the broker to change from the July to the April order? The brokers on the floor might say, "Do the same thing in April."

You should say:

Buy 2 XYZ Apr 50 calls at 3 and cancel to buy 2 XYZ July 50 calls at 3.

Since the market has a way of surprising even the most astute investor, it pays to trade with a contingency plan in mind. Remember "‡¢@*&8. %☆+"3•*@/—#†©÷'5$#§-/®★○‡•0%;¢@™6". Built into this plan should be a point at which you will quit when you're ahead or cut your losses when you're behind.

After you have invested and have either exercised your option, sold it in the secondary market, or allowed it to expire without a profit, you will calculate the return or loss on your investment. This is a very important step because it allows you to see how close or far you are from your goals. This is the function of your account maintenance notebook. It will remind you at all times where you are in relationship to the intended route. Account maintenance will be an ongoing part of your operation. Make sure you balance your own accounts with the monthly statements that you will receive from your broker, in the same way you balance your checkbook. Good record keeping is essential. Keep a notebook especially for this purpose. Write your trades down rather than leaving them to memory. Record the date, time, contract, striking price, broker transaction number, expiration date, cost of the option, and cost of commission. Over time this notebook will develop into a picture of your trading activities and supply a trading overview. In addition, your notes will provide an indication of how certain options contracts tend to trade over a period of time, and if you continue to trade other options contracts, you will increase your awareness of the market pulse overall. Give yourself a certain amount of time each month for this important function. As you become more sophisticated, you may want to refer to indicators such as yield curves, the models of Black-Scholes or Kassouf.

On this trek you should also keep a personal journal. If you keep it honestly and diligently (do not editorialize; remember, you *can* fool yourself) and study it carefully, it can be a gold mine in self-discovery and hence an invaluable aid in trading (and life). Sometimes your record of performance may tell you that you do not want to trade over *x* dollar amount, that your performance seems to deteriorate if you go above that sum; or you may discover exactly the opposite, that you do better when larger amounts are at stake. Who knows? That's why you keep a personal performance chart in the first place. Your journal might dictate that you want to change your approach, or on the other hand it might tell you something you never even realized but became aware of after looking at your performance objectively. You may discover your success in the market is influenced by some psychological ingredient triggered by some heretofore undetected mechanism; for example, you may discover you trade better after a relaxing weekend or, conversely, when you are under pressure. Such detail will only emerge if you keep an emotional journal as well as a maintenance log, which brings us to *the* important point.

After placing your order, the primary concern becomes, Will the trade make money? Before money can be made, the trade must first reach its break-even point. Meaning theoretically that if the premium cost $500 ($5 per share on 100 shares), then the option will have to trade for 5 points, or $500, in order for the trade to break even, not counting commissions and taxes. Now to the practical. (When you include commissions and taxes, you will find the trade has to go a bit past 5 points—maybe even to 5½ points—before breaking even.) After break-even come profits, and profits are what everyone is in the game for.

The conventional Moolahnite axiom is "Buy the rumor, sell the news," but remember . . . profits can be made on both sides of the market. Though rallies tend to attract the attention of most investors, don't forget that through the power of the put, there is still money to be made when the market drops. In fact, there is an entire school of trading, contrarian, devoted to going against the grain. Contrarian-theory traders profit by making a general practice of trading opposite to popular market trends and opinion. Whatever works and from wherever it comes, take all the help you can get.

Speaking of help, I asked an acquaintance who had suddenly done well in the Options Game how he was enjoying his newly acquired wealth. He seemed not to be enjoying himself. I asked what the problem was. He explained that his family did not seem to be enjoying his success. The solution to his problem hit me almost as soon as he said the words. He had said *his* success and not *our* success. The big mistake he had made was not including his family in the process.

My friend did not share his struggle with his family and in return his family did not give him the support he felt he deserved. How could they when they didn't have a sense of participation? This oversight is not unusual. Curious, sad, ironic, but not unusual. We often inadvertently overlook the most important form of help, our loved ones, which in most cases is the major motive for entering the fray in the first place. Many people who are achievers are so busy developing and working their programs for success that they simply forget that the family wants to participate. Now, you may ask yourself . . . Should you the breadwinner who has always been the family's strength, who always makes the investment decisions alone, based on your hard-learned knowledge (which often even had to be explained to you by the financial adviser, accountant, or some financial mind greater than your own), should you burden your loved ones? Yes and no. Yes, you should bring them into your activities, but no, not as a *burden,* as an *opportunity.* Will the family be interested in all this mumbo jumbo . . . of puts and calls? Since there is no substitute for action, and no surprise like life itself . . . there is only one way to find out, ask the family. You may be surprised.

Not only will you gain their admiration but you might gain a convert and unearth a latent talent in one of your very own unsuspecting family members. Human nature wants to be a part of the action. Perhaps your professional occupation does not allow for this participation. Options do. This is not a new idea. The team concept is as old as the cave dwellers who banded together to defeat the great woolly mammoth. And executives in the largest corporations today still follow this old tried-and-true approach. Each person in the family will learn at their own rate, and in this case the concept of "each one teach one" may prove itself invaluable beyond your expectations. The feeling of doing something together or striving for a common goal can not only bring the family closer together but can also provide the training ground for a career as well.

But be careful not to mask the reality of your struggle from them. Keep in mind participation should not be made to look like a grand game, but a serious financial challenge. The family that struggles together stays together.

Part of this family struggle should be setting limits and goals. If, for instance, your goal is to invest five hundred dollars per month, you might be surprised to find that your children are willing to forgo that new minibike or television set to help the family make its goal. With the family at your side and Lady Luck on your shoulder, swing for the bleachers.

11

FINE POINTS

Until the introduction in 1981 of a pilot options program on treasury bonds by the Commodity Futures Trading Commission, stock options had been the darling of the Options Game. So successful was this new experimental program that more options futures games were allowed to develop, such as options on futures contracts in the gold, silver, and sugar markets.

However, to the general surprise of Wall Street (though not in hindsight, mind you; the Moolahnites all swear they knew it all the time) a completely different kind of option ascended to popularity, a mutation based on an index. These index options, these emerging clear winners, are truly revolutionary in that they do not even have an underlying asset. And the winner among the winners is the Options Index, based on the Standard &

Poor's (S&P) 100 Index, which is a stock index. An index is the average prices of a group of stocks, and unlike an options contract with a tangible underlying asset, an index option is settled in either corresponding futures contracts or cash. Other index options include the AMEX's Major Market and Market Value, the New York Stock Exchange's Composite Stock Exchange Index (NYSE), Value Line Index, and the gold and silver traded in Philadelphia. A major shot in the arm for options indexes was a governmental windfall allowing options index profits to be taxed at a maximum of 32 percent rather than the 50 percent maximum allowed for stock options.

The S&P 100 Stock Index options began trading in 1983 on the Chicago Board of Trade and to date they are doing tremendous business. Their volume is more than all of the listed options on the AMEX combined.

The mechanics of index options work the same as for other options. One hundred blue-chip stocks currently listed on the CBOE comprise the S&P 100 Index. The S&P 100 Index is computed by taking the market price of each of the stocks in the index and multiplying that by the number of outstanding shares of the stock. The values are then added to determine the combined market value of the stocks which makes up the S&P 100 Index. The market value is then divided by the base value and multiplied by 100. Though changes in the base value continue to be adjusted to reflect mergers, acquisitions, stock rights, splits, substitutions or changes in capitalization, each point represents $100. For example, if an options buyer purchased a 155 April call in February at 3 when the index was trading at 158 and sold the call for 8 on March 30 when the index was trading at 163, the call buyer would be $500 richer.

COMPOSITION OF THE S&P 100 STOCK INDEX*

Aluminum Co. of America
American Electric Power
American Express
American Hospital Supply
American Telephone & Telegraph
AMP
Atlantic Richfield
Avon Products
BankAmerica
Baxter Travenol Labs
Bethlehem Steel
Black & Decker
Boeing
Boise Cascade
Bristol-Myers
Brunswick
Burlington Northern
Burroughs
Champion International
CIGNA
Citicorp
Coca-Cola
Colgate-Palmolive
Commonwealth Edison
Computer Sciences
Control Data
Datapoint
Delta Airlines
Digital Equipment
Disney Productions
Dow Chemical
duPont
Eastman Kodak
Exxon
Fluor
Ford Motor
General Dynamics
General Electric
General Foods
General Motors
Great Western Financial
Gulf + Western
Halliburton
Harris
Hewlett-Packard

*This list reflects the composition of the index as of January 1985. The composition changes over time.

Holiday Corp.
Homestake Mining
Honeywell
Hughes Tool
Humana
IBM
International Flavors & Fragrances
International Minerals & Chemicals
International Paper
International Telephone & Telegraph
Johnson & Johnson
K-Mart
Litton Industries
McDonald's
Merck
Merrill Lynch
Minnesota Mining & Mfg.
Mobil
Monsanto
National Semiconductor
NCR
Norfolk Southern
Northern Telecom Ltd.
Northwest Airlines
Northwest Industries
Occidental Petroleum
Owens-Illinois
PepsiCo
Polaroid
Ralston Purina
Raytheon
RCA
Revlon
R. J. Reynolds
Rockwell International
Safeway Stores
Schlumberger
Sears, Roebuck
Skyline
Sperry
Squibb
Storage Technology
Tandy
Tektronix
Teledyne
Texas Instruments
UAL
Upjohn
United Technologies
Wal-Mart Stores
Warner Communications
Weyerhaeuser
Williams
Xerox

According to the CBOE, the S&P 100's success can be attributed in large part to the versatility of the contract in that it appeals to a broad range of investment goals, "from the conservative blue chip equity investor seeking to reduce market risk to the more aggresssive investor willing to speculate and assume a higher degree of risk." This includes "the market risk involved in stock portfolio ownership," which again falls within the parameters of large institutional investors.

Options based on indexes, of whatever, offer the investor the luxury of staying in the game without added risk. In the buying or selling of a futures contract there is unlimited risk (in the buying of stocks also) plus the dollar intensity. This brings us back to the benefit of dealing only in the buying of options, which I cannot repeat too often, that the buyer of an option is only at limited risk for the amount of the premium, and there is never any margin call.

Once indexes caught on, they began to proliferate. Some indexes have a specialized narrow base, such as transportation, oil, and high technology, and some are more broadly based, such as AMEX Major Market and the S&P 100. The narrow-based indexes have not been as popular. The current theory in vogue is that the narrow-based indexes do not have the confidence of the bigger institutional investors who do not feel safe hedging large stock positions with them.

No matter what the option is based on, whether it is stocks, commodities, financial instruments, or indexes, it is imperative that you read and understand the financial section of the newspaper as well as stock tickers and other market reports, for this will enable you to check on your investments daily and allow you to understand events and movements in the larger financial community.

READING FINANCIAL DATA

READING STOCK AND OPTIONS TABLES

The stock tables are listed in the *New York Times* as follows:

52-Week High	Low	Stock	Div	Yld %	PE Ratio	Sales 100s	High	Low	Last	Chg

High the highest price the stock reached in the last 12 months

Low the lowest price at which the stock traded in the last 12 months

Stock the stock's name (or abbreviation)

Div the dividend per share that the stock paid

Yld % the percentage return represented by the annual dividend at the current stock price

PE Ratio the price/earnings ratio

Sales 100s the amount of sales in 100s that took place during that day

High the highest price at which the stock traded on that day

Low the lowest price traded on that day
If the stock traded between a high of 52 and a low of 48¾, the *range* of that stock for that day would be 3¼.

Last the closing price of the stock on that day

Chg the difference in the price of that day's closing from the *previous* day's closing price. If on Wednesday IBM closed at 130, and on Thursday it closed at 130¼, the net change in Friday's paper would indicate + ¼.

Stock tables are one thing, and options tables are another. Options tables differ from stock tables in that they will list the put and call prices on various options. Since it's the newest and the biggest, let's go with the flow and use the S&P 100 Index options table for our options example.

S&P 100 INDEX

Option & NY Close	Strike Price	Calls—Last May-Jun-Jul			Puts—Last May-Jun-Jul		
S&P							
176.96	160	17¾	r	19¾	r	r	⅛
176.96	165	12⅝	13⅝	r	1/16	⅛	¼
176.96	170	7½	9	11	⅛	½	13/16
176.96	175	3¼	5⅛	6⅞	1	1¾	2⅛
176.96	180	15/16	2½	4	3⅝	4⅜	4⅝

OPTION
the name of the company or the company's abbreviation (XYZ) (in the case of an index, the index name)

NY CLOSE
the day's closing price

STRIKE PRICE
the price at which the option can be exercised

CALLS—LAST
closing price for the call option

MONTH LISTED
the expiration date of the option

PUTS—LAST
the closing price for the put option

r
indicates that the option was not traded

Although the format may change slightly from one publication to another, the meanings of the terms will remain constant. The companies listed in the newspaper can be identified by their abbreviations. Your broker may be able to supply you with a booklet listing company names and their abbreviations. You will also find listed on the financial pages such information as categories listing new highs, new lows, dividends, corporate earnings, most active stocks, and open-interest statistics.

READING THE TICKER TAPE

The stock ticker tape has two printing positions, an upper line and a lower line. The upper line carries the alphabetical abbreviation of the stock and other lettered transaction information, while the lower line carries only numerical information concerning prices and volume. Sales are recorded according to the units the stocks are traded in, and 100 shares represents the usual unit size.

Sales of 100 shares are indicated by the price of the shares, omitting the volume. Example:

XYZ
550

When a sale of 100 shares occurs and the price is a number with a fraction of 1/16 or less, the unit of volume is indicated by the number, followed by the symbol *s*, followed by price. Example:

XYZ
1s4.1.16

In sales of more than 100 but less than 1,000 shares (where the unit of trading is 100 shares), volume is indicated by the first digit or whole number, followed by *s*, followed by price.

Example: A sale of 200 shares of XYZ at 25 would appear:

XYZ
2s25

Sales of more than 1,000 but less than 10,000 (where the unit of trading is 100 shares) are indicated by printing the number of groups of shares of 100, followed by *s*, followed by price. Example: A sale of 4,000 shares of XYZ at 25 would appear:

XYZ
40s25

Units of less than 100 shares traded on a 10-, 25-, or 50-unit basis are indicated by printing the actual number of shares followed by *ss*, followed by the price.

Example: A sale of 10 shares of XYZ at 25 would appear:

XYZ
10ss25

Digits and fractions of price are usually printed in full.

Example: A sale of 300 shares of XYZ at 25⅜ would appear:

XYZ
3s25⅜

A sale of 300 shares of XYZ at 7³⁄₁₆ would appear:

XYZ
3s7.3.16

Multiple sales are printed without repeating alphabetical symbols, but by separating each transaction by two dots on the lower line.

Example: A sale of 400 shares of XYZ at 40 followed by a sale of 600 shares of XYZ at 40⅛ would read:

XYZ
4s40..6s40⅛

Variations increase as transactions gain complexity, but this should give you enough understanding to get you out of the dark and into the light.

MARKET INDICATORS

The age-old question on everyone's lips always seems to be the same. What's going to happen next? Each Moolahnite, of course, will tell you they have just the right answers. Then each will proceed to explain the market according to a pet theory. Of course, the real truth is that no one really knows. In order to buttress themselves against the fears of the great unknown, Wall Streeters have devised a thousand theoretical and systematic models to analyze the market and foresee the future. Ultimately, market analysis became accepted as true religion. Some of the cults preach that on occasion, through the faith of investor confidence, they have the power to influence the market. The raw material for market analysis, the building blocks used in these models and theories, are called market indicators.

DOW JONES

Foremost among the indicators are the stock price average indexes based on the theory of Charles H. Dow, a founder of the Dow Jones Company and the first editor of *The Wall Street Journal*. Dow theorized that the trend of the market could be expressed in the movement of twenty stocks, called the Dow Jones Railroad Average, and twelve other stocks representing other types of industry, called the Dow Jones Industrial Average (DJIA). Over the years various stocks have fallen from grace, some to disappear forever into the great void, only to be replaced by brash newcomers. Anyway, in 1928 the DJIA was expanded to include thirty stocks and remains at that number today. The stocks which currently make up the Dow Jones Industrial Average are:*

Allied Chemical
Alcoa
American Brands
American Can
American Express
American Telephone & Telegraph
Bethlehem Steel

*Daily stock price record, New York Stock Exchange, March 1985.

Chevron Corp.
duPont
Eastman Kodak
Exxon
General Electric
General Foods
General Motors
Goodyear
Inco Ltd.
International Business Machines (IBM)
International Harvester
International Paper
Merck & Co.
Minnesota Mining & Manufacturing Co.
Owens-Ill Glass
Procter & Gamble
Sears, Roebuck
Texaco
Union Carbide
United Technologies
U S Steel
Westinghouse Electric
Woolworth

Adding twenty transportation stocks and fifteen utility stocks to the thirty industrials, Dow constructed the Dow Jones Stock Average consisting of sixty-five stocks. However, the Dow Jones thirty industrials is the most popular and widely used indicator to date.

On April 27, 1985, the *New York Times* listing read:

DOW JONES STOCK AVERAGES

	Open	*High*	*Low*	*Close*	*Chg*
30 Industrials	1286.22	1290.30	1270.54	1275.18	−9.60
20 Transports	592.45	594.77	583.81	586.25	−6.64
15 Utilities	154.95	155.47	153.98	154.75	−0.10
65 Stocks	518.12	519.88	511.93	513.98	−3.85

In the above example the net change of −9.60 is not a percentage, nor is it dollars and cents, but a figure based on the actual price movement of the stock divided by the Dow Jones divisor. Many financial reports on electronic media quote the Dow Jones Stock Averages on a daily basis.

In 1972 on November 14th, the Dow Jones Industrial Average reached 1003.16, surpassing the seemingly unattainable 1000 mark; that is, for the first time in history the average price of the thirty industrial stocks was over 1000. As the industrial average continues to rise, the magic mark is projected higher and higher (sort of a four-minute-mile syndrome in reverse).

STANDARD & POOR'S INDEX

The Standard & Poor's Index, commonly called the S&P, was introduced in 1957. This index consists of five hundred stocks, representing a broader base than the Dow Jones Index. The stock averages are comprised of four hundred industrials, twenty transportation, forty utilities, and forty financials. Because it consists of more issues, it shows a lower percentage of fluctuation, and is considered by some investment professionals a better index than the Dow Jones.

THE NEW YORK STOCK EXCHANGE INDEX

The NYSE Index consists of all the common stocks listed on the New York Stock Exchange (no preferred shares). This index was introduced in 1966. It consists of over five hundred issues.

The Dow Jones, the Standard & Poor's, and the New York Stock Exchange indexes all appear together in the

New York Times financial section under the market indicator column. The adherence to indexes is based on the premise that the averaging of a group of stocks can better signify a primary up-or-down price trend in the market than a single asset. As stated before, analyzing the market is a major concern for the investment-minded. Moolahnites thrive on finding increasingly bizarre market indicators as fodder for their theories and models. Just what these indicators *really do* signify is a completely different kettle of fish. In fact, the arguments of just what indicators indicate are so dogmatic someone got the bright idea of inventing a new Options Game around the newest indicator game, the then-recent game of futures indexes. In other words, the options index game, take a deep breath, is a game based on a game based on an index. That (whether the Moolahnites admit it or not) is how the options index game was born.

MARKET ANALYSIS

Until about fifteen years ago there were two dominant approaches to determining how to best forecast the stock market, that of the fundamentalist and that of the technician.

THE FUNDAMENTAL APPROACH

The fundamentalist believes that the market is a rational entity and that clues and answers to how a company's stock should or will be trading can be found by close examination of its financial picture through the use of sophisticated accounting, business, and economic yardsticks. Questions as to (1) expected future earnings, (2) expected future dividends, (3) the asset value, (4) the price/earnings ratio, (5) the method for valuing expected earnings, (6) the company's market share, (7) the company's past earnings, (8) return on equity ratio, (9) pretax return on sales are asked by the fundamentalists, and (10) debt to equity ratio. This method is popular with many lending institutions.

THE TECHNICAL APPROACH

The technical theorist feels that all of the important information is reflected in the price of the company's stock and believes that getting a handle on the direction of future price movements is the key to the kingdom. In *Contrarian Investment Strategy* Joseph Granville, a leading technical analyst gospelizer, explains that

> technicians look ahead, fundamentalists look backwards. The true language of the market is technical . . . the majority of those involved in the market are bombarded with mistimed fundamental data which nine times out of ten haven't a blessed thing to do with where the price of stock or the market is headed.

The tools of the technicians are charts reflecting price changes from one time period to the next. These price-movement charts show recurring patterns that the technician interprets and translates into support and resistance buy or sell signals. The language used to describe these patterns includes (1) head and shoulders, (2) diamond wedges, (3) fan movements, (4) double bottoms, and (5) flags flying at half-mast.

And then there are even those who believe that, well . . .

RANDOM WALK APPROACH

At the turn of the century a French mathematician, Louis Bachelier, presented in his doctoral thesis on prices of commodities and government bonds evidence that there was no conclusive link between past price behavior and future price performance. In 1963 Clive Granger and Oskar Morgenstern turned their researching talents toward the subject of price movement, using the mathematical technique of spectral analysis. Arnold Moore did a price movement study in 1964, and Eugene Fama conducted related research in 1965. Interestingly enough, all of the research pointed back to the original findings some sixty years earlier of Bachelier, that there is no connection between past and future price behavior. Thus was born the random walk theory, which holds that prices tend to move randomly, following no predictable pattern or design. This theory refutes both the technicians and the fundamentalists, and has developed its own following among professional investors.

But be it fundamental, technical, random, or women's hemlines, the Moolahnites, like the lottery player and the old lady at the one-armed bandit, will continue searching for relationships and clues to the question of what's going to happen next in the market.

NICETIES

Details are fascinating, and here are a few.

EX-DIVIDEND

The term often used to refer to the dividend is "*ex-dividend*." The term means without dividend.

According to Rule 956 of the Floor Transaction Handbook of the AMEX:

> No adjustment is made to any of the terms of Exchange traded puts or calls to reflect the declaration or payment of cash distributions made out of earnings and profits. However, if the holder of the call exercises it prior to an exdate for a distribution, the exercising holder is entitled to the dividend. Conversely, the holder of a put who exercises it prior to an exdate must also deliver the distribution to the writer even though the underlying security might be delivered after the exdate.

STOCK SPLITS

A stock split occurs thereby increasing the number of shares outstanding and thus can affect the price of the option. For example, if XYZ Corporation split its shares on a 2 to 1 basis, one option originally covering 100 shares at $60 per share would be transformed into two options on XYZ that reflect 200 shares of XYZ Corporation at $30 per share.

Similarly, if the stock split was 3 to 2, instead of covering 100 shares of stock at the exercise price of $60 per share, the original option would adjust to $40 per share to reflect 150 shares of XYZ.

Another example of a change in the original option could occur if XYZ was acquired in a merger, for cash, in which case an option may be adjusted from $60 per share, representing 100 shares upon delivery, to $6,000 in cash.

This chart indicates the more frequent distribution for stock splits.

Distribution	**Price of Order Divided by**
5 for 4	1.25
4 for 3	1.33
3 for 2	1.50
5 for 3	1.66
2 for 1	2.00
5 for 2	2.50
3 for 1	3.00
4 for 1	4.00

CURRENCY OPTIONS

The possible variations on the Options Game seem to be inexhaustible. There are options on currency, the aforementioned deutsche marks, for example. There are options on gold and silver, which are traded more as commodities than as currency. Now there are options on Eurodollars. (Technically, Eurodollars are dollars held by foreigners, although not necessarily European. There are three kinds of Eurodollars: One type is money which can be called upon on a day's notice with no fixed date of maturity. Another is a million-dollar certificate of deposit, and the third is a million-dollar 90-day time deposit.) A new wrinkle has been added to the Options Game by the Philadelphia Exchange, which, hoping to attract the large foreign segment of Eurodollar speculators, has started a Eurodollar Options Game to compete with the Chicago game by adding a feature of the European method of options trading which does not allow an option to be exercised before expiration.

THE BLACK-SCHOLES MODEL

Many investors who'll want to get knee-deep in options will no doubt be aided by the mathematical formulas that have come to be associated with options. Probably the most popular has been the Black-Scholes Model. This model was developed around 1973, close to the introduction of CBOE's listed options.

This basic formula has been altered by many other theorists and computerists, but it still serves as a popular basic options formula.

The variables in the evaluation are:

p = stock price
s = striking price
t = time remaining until expiration expressed as a percent of the year
r = current risk-free interest
v = volatility measured by annual standard deviation

ln = natural logarithm
N(X) = cumulative normal density function

The delta (the amount the option price can be expected to change in relation to the stock) or the hedge ratio is a by-product of the Black-Scholes Model.

$$\text{Theoretical option price} = pN\,(d_1) - se^{-rt}N\,(d_2)$$

$$\text{where } d_1 = \frac{\ln\left(\frac{p}{s}\right) + \left(r + \frac{v^2}{2}\right)t}{v\sqrt{t}}$$

$$d_2 = d_1 - v\sqrt{t}$$

$$Delta = N\,(d_1)$$

This formula can be easily programmed into a programmable calculator or computer.

This formula does not take dividends into consideration. Its critics declare that one of the big unknowns that the model doesn't seem to fully encompass is the question of volatility (i.e., to what extent the market will fluctuate over a given period).

The four options actions:

OPENING

	CALL		**PUT**
Buyer	Pay call price	**Buyer**	Deliver underlying security
	Receive call		Receive put

Seller	Receive call price Deliver call	**Seller**	Receive put price Deliver put

EXERCISE

Buyer	Pay exercise price Deliver call Receive underlying security	**Buyer**	Deliver underlying security Deliver put Receive exercise price
Seller	Receive exercise price Receive call Deliver underlying security	**Seller**	Receive underlying security Receive put Pay exercise price

CLOSING

Buyer	Pay call price Receive call	**Buyer**	Pay put price Receive put
Seller	Receive call price Deliver call	**Seller**	Receive put price Deliver put

EXPIRE
(out-of-the-money)

Buyer	No action	**Buyer**	No action
Seller	Not affected	**Seller**	Not affected

MECHANICS OF EXERCISE

Once a writer of the option is exercised, he must deliver, as mandated by the Options Clearing Corporation (OCC). The OCC exercises the firm on a random-selection basis, and the firm in turn chooses the customers to be assigned the exercise notices. The firm must specify in the options agreement how it will make options exercise assignments. It may do so on a random basis, or it may choose to do so on the FIFO principle (first in, first out).

Just as the OCC has established position limits (i.e., prohibiting ownership of more than a certain amount of options contracts on any one side of the market) to discourage manipulation of the market by large investors, it has also established exercise limits for similar purposes. This means that no more than a certain amount of contracts of the same class may be exercised in any five business days.

BELL CURVE

The distribution of stock prices is based on logarithmical distribution using a bell-shaped curve.

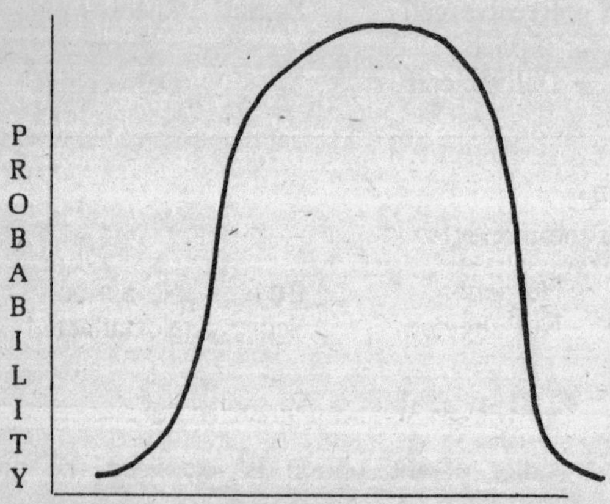

Bell Curve

Almost any theory can be transformed into a sophisticated-looking formula. For instance, remember I mentioned annualized risk earlier? This is the formula:

$$\text{Annualized risk} + \sum_i \text{INV}_i \frac{360}{H_i}$$

where INV_i = percent of total assets invested in options with holding periods, H_i

where H_i = length of holding period in total days.

The extent to which the models and formulas actually reflect the real world has been a subject for debate among both academicians and market professionals. But remember, mathematical theorists are people, too, and are in the same boat as the economist, the political scientist, the perfume maker, or you and I. The theorist, after all is said and done, is simply using mathematical approximations to try and predict the course of the real world, much in the same way a politician constructs a platform on what he hopes people will vote for, or the way a perfume maker chooses a fragrance, based on what he thinks people will buy.

In the end it all comes down to trying to approximate the actions of people in the real world by whatever discipline one chooses.

. . . Why not take the shortcut up the mountainside, you say, instead of hacking our way through the jungle? . . . Looks easier, anyway? Oh, yeah . . . Notice those funny white branches all along that mountain path? Well, those are not branches, friend, those are skeletons . . . the bones of impatient investors. They had the same shortcut idea. The trail is not impassable, but it takes experience and expensive equipment. One day maybe . . . not yet anyway.

12

DON'TS (NOT YET ANYWAY)

STOCKS

Although the focus of this book is not on stocks (stocks are capital-intensive, slow-moving, and carry unlimited risk, without the benefits of the leverage that options offer), a discussion of the following strategies will be beneficial, because stocks are the genesis of much of the trading logic and coincidentally the asset with which the layperson is most familiar and the primary vehicle through which most people were introduced to the financial marketplace.

PURCHASING

When an investor purchases stock, the profit or loss possibility simply lies in the price fluctuations that will take place from the day that he purchases. If the investor were to purchase 100 shares of stock at $10 per share for a total price of $1,000, and if the stock were to go to $15 per share, the investor's $1,000 investment would become worth $1,500 (100 shares at $15 per share). On the other hand, if the price were to fall to $7 per share, the original investment of $1,000 would only be worth $700 (100 shares at $7 per share). Adjustments would be necessary to reflect dividends earned, in which case the investor would adjust by raising the dollar value of his investment by the amount of the dividend. If, for instance, the dividend paid on the first year was .20 per share on 100 shares and at the end of the first year the stock was still selling at the buying price of $10 per share, then the total worth of the original $1,000 investment would become $1,020. Two additional adjustments would be required, one for reduction of the profit by the amount of commissions paid to the broker for his services buying and selling the stock, and the other for taxes.

SELLING SHORT

The term "short" means not having, as in "I wanted to see the movie but I was short two dollars." An investor sells when he thinks that a stock will go lower than its current price. He sells a stock he does not own with the intention of buying it back at a lower price. The natural question that arises here is how can he sell something he doesn't own. Simple. The short-seller borrows the stock from someone else, then sells it. If he sells the stock short at $10 per share and if the price declines to $8, the short-seller would purchase the stock for $8 per share and the result would be exactly the same as if the stock had been bought for $8 and sold for $10, with a $2 profit on the transaction. Only the order is reversed. Adjustments on the short sale would be different from adjustments on a stock purchase transaction. Since it was necessary to borrow the stock in the first place, the short-seller has to pay to the original owner any dividends the stock might have earned while he held it. This charge is interest that the short-seller pays to the original owner of the stock. Even so, the short-seller is still liable to the broker for commissions from the sale as well as for any taxes that will be assessed in the profits after adjustments.

PURCHASING STOCK ON MARGIN

The purpose of buying stock on margin is to increase the investor's leverage. Buying on margin simply means buying on credit. A margin account or credit arrangement is set up between the customer and a brokerage house. The brokerage house asks the customer to put up part of the purchase price of a stock and charges him interest for "lending" him the balance. The usual arrangement is that the brokerage house lends the customer 50 percent of the stock price. Let us suppose 100 shares of stock were bought on margin at $10 per share. The customer would pay in $500 and the brokerage house would pay in $500, with an interest charge of 10 percent per year. If at the end of the year the stock remained at $10 per share, the customer would now owe the brokerage company $550 ($500 original loan plus $50 interest owed).

SELLING SHORT ON MARGIN

The sale of stock short on margin is very similar to a regular sale of stock short, except that the transaction is made on credit. The interest required for a long sale is not required for a short sale. The margin requirement guarantees that the short-seller will live up to his contract if the stock should rise instead of fall.

PURCHASING A STOCK AND SELLING A PUT

The investor owns the stock and is betting that the stock will go up. The selling of the put is simply another bet that the stock is going up. This strategy offers no downside protection and in fact doubles the downside risk, because for every dollar that the stock moves downward in value, the investor on this strategy is losing dollar for dollar on the long stock position and begins losing 2 to 1 past the point of the premium dollar value received for the put. Usually an investor who employs this strategy doesn't mind being the owner of a great deal of the stock even if the value is low.

PURCHASING THE STOCK AND PURCHASING A PUT

The investor in this case can participate fully in any upward move of the stock, and the purchase of the put provides the investor with downside protection should the market plummet. The maximum loss to the investor from the option would be the premium of the put.

PURCHASING A STOCK AND SELLING A CALL

This strategy is that of a covered-call writer. The term "covered" is used because the seller of the call has also purchased the stock. By selling a call one can buy a series of downside protection plateaus to the extent that the downside move doesn't amount to more than the premium received for the sale of the call. The sale of a call against that stock offers a profit to the seller, but limits the upside potential of the investment while providing limited downside protection.

SELLING SHORT AND PURCHASING A CALL

This strategy is similar to the former except that it is done with different instruments. The purchase of the call gives unlimited upside protection while the short sale enables the investor to reap any potential should the market drop substantially. Remember, however, that the market still has to drop enough to cover the cost of the call premium before the short-seller sees a profit.

STRATEGIES

These strategies are not so complex that you will not master them in due time, but venturing into these areas at the beginning of your trading career would tie up prohibitive amounts of capital in the form of commissions and margins to carry the positions. Not to mention that most strategies need experience—experience in the feel of the market's peculiarities, pitfalls, and pulse. Some might say that to include these strategies in your options arsenal at the outset is no more than simple conventional wisdom, but conventional wisdom (Oh, Grandmother, what big teeth you have!) is usually a convenient meal for someone else. However, believing as Freud said that the unknown is the biggest fear, a look at some of the commonplace as well as more esoteric strategies is provided just so they will not remain cloaked in mystery. Stick to our path . . . only buy puts or calls. This peek behind the door is only to familiarize you with the dangers that lurk . . . remember . . . DON'T!

NAKED (UNCOVERED) CALL WRITING (SELLING)

This involves the selling of a call to a buyer. For example, if one were to sell a June 40 call on 100 shares of XYZ, the seller would collect a premium from the buyer without actually owning the 100 shares. In this case, the seller is collecting a premium from the buyer and betting that on the June expiration date of the option, the XYZ stock will be selling below $40 per share.

This strategy is called uncovered or naked writing because if at the June expiration date the stock is selling above $40, the seller has to then go out into the open market and buy the stock at the market price.

Remember Ned and Harvey? For example, if instead of apples Ned sells Harvey a June 40 call option on 100 shares of XYZ for $500 ($5 per share), Ned is betting that upon the June expiration date XYZ will be selling for less than $45 per share and he'll get to keep the premium of $500 and count it as a profit. If, however, on the other hand, upon the June expiration date the XYZ stock is selling for $46 per share, Harvey will most likely exercise his right to buy the stock at $40. At this point, Ned must go into the market and buy the XYZ stock at $46 per share.

Ned's outcome would be:

	Rec'd	Paid
Call premium	500	
Stock cost		(4600)
Sold to Harvey	4000	
Ned's net loss		(100)

Harvey's net outcome would be:

Harvey (paid for option)		(500)
Bought from Ned		(4000)
Sold stock at $46 per share	4600	
Harvey's net gain	100	

However, at the price of $46 Harvey does not necessarily have to exercise his right to buy the stock at $40 per share from Ned but might rather choose simply to sell the call for which he paid $500 to someone else before the expiration date for (let's assume he is lucky), say, $850, thus accruing a $350 profit.

Ned as the call writer has unlimited liability because the stock could theoretically go up forever.

NAKED (UNCOVERED) PUT WRITING (SELLING)

A put *buyer* makes his purchase thinking that the stock will go down. The put *seller* makes his money (premium) if the market stays the same or goes up. The seller takes the money from the buyer on the agreement that if the stock stays the same or goes higher, he (as the seller) gets to keep the premium paid by the buyer. When the put seller makes this kind of arrangement with a buyer, and does not in fact own the stock, the put is described as being sold "naked" or "uncovered."

SPREADING

Spreading is a system that takes advantage of the pricing relationships between two or more securities or commodities. A spreader is not so much concerned about the market price of one entity as about the pricing relationship between the entities.

There are many different kinds of spreading strategies. There are spreads involving purchase and sale of the same class of options with the same strike prices but with different expiration dates. Then there are spreads with different strike prices and with the same expiration dates and can be done with either puts or calls, and there are spreads with names ranging from the Butterfly to the Bull.

During the early 1970s when options became more attractive, many traders with sharp pencils and quick minds entered the game, resulting in clever machinations geared to take advantage of even the smallest quirks in the marketplace. The complexity and combination of tactics can be mind-boggling. Nevertheless, they are the tools with which countless traders have made—and lost—fortunes.

Calendar Spread

When a trader buys a spread, he does so in the hopes that as the expiration date nears, the numerical relationship of the options purchased will have changed in value to the point of allowing a profit.

Stock	*Strike*	**Nov** Call	**Nov** Put	**Feb** Call	**May** Call	**Last** Price
XYZ	50	5	2¾	6½	8	53
XYZ	55	2¾	5	3¼	3½	53

The spreader decides to *buy* 1 Feb 50 call @ 6½ and *sell* 1 Nov 50 call @ 5 for a debit or cost of *1½*.

Let us suppose that near the Nov expiration date the XYZ stock is selling at 48. The Nov 50 call, which has no intrinsic value, is therefore selling at ¼, and the Feb 50 call is selling at 3, because there is still time value to the Feb option (but no intrinsic value). To close out the position, the spreader will place an order to buy a Nov 50 call at ¼ and sell the Feb 50 call at 3 for a credit of 2¾. The spreader now deducts the original debit of 1½ from the credit of 2¼ for a net profit of ¾ on the trade.

This kind of spread is called a time or calendar spread because it involves the simultaneous purchase and sale of options within the same class but with different expiration dates.

Bull Spread

A bull spread is executed if the investor thinks the market will move up. The investor buys a call at one striking price and sells a call at a higher striking price for a debit. Usually both options have the same expiration date. This position can be profitable if the market moves up. It is therefore a bullish outlook. This spread has limited potential and limited risks. For example, if XYZ stock is trading at 37, the July 35 call at 3, and the July 40 call at 1, a bull spread could be established by purchasing the July 35 and simultaneously selling the July 40 for a 2-point debit. The bull spread will have a debit on the basis that the lower striking price trades for more than the higher striking price. The spread maximizes its profit if at expiration date the stock is trading at or over the higher striking price of 40. The maximum loss occurs if at expiration date the stock is trading under the lower strike price of 35 and is equal to 2 points.

The break-even point on this spread would be at 37 (the lower strike price of 35 plus the debit of 2 = 37). The maximum profit of 3 would be higher strike price 40 minus lower strike of 35 minus debit of 2 = 3. In order to understand the potential outcome, a buyer should calculate commission costs before position is established.

Bear Spread

The bear spread is for the investor who expects the market to go lower. The bear spreader will sell the higher priced option which has the lower striking price, and buy the lower priced option having the higher striking price. This spread will result in a credit to the investor establishing the position. For example:

XYZ stock selling @ 37
Sell Jul 35 call @ 3
Buy Jul 40 call @ 1

The credit will be 2 points.

The spreader is hoping that both options will expire worthless, and will have maximized his profit potential by pocketing the money received from the credit of 2 points. Because it is a credit position from the outset, it is a somewhat popular strategy.

Butterfly Spread

A butterfly spread is a combination of both a bull and a bear spread. This spread involves three striking prices and consists of buying one call at a high striking price, selling two calls at a middle striking price, and buying another call at the lower striking price. The butterfly can also be achieved by selling options at the lowest and highest striking prices and buying them at the middle striking price. This strategy is for the investor who thinks the market will remain neutral. Maximum profit is derived at the middle striking price.

Remember how Moolahnites love models and formulas? What do you say we take a break for a minute and instead of doing aerobics, glance at the formula for the butterfly spread? Lawrence McMillan's book *Options as a Strategic Investment* presents it as follows:

D = downside break-even point
P = maximum profit potential
R = maximum risk potential
U = upside break-even point
s = striking price
c = call price
p = put price

A butterfly spread combines a bull spread using strikes s_1 and s_2 with a bear spread using strikes s_2 and s_3.

$s_1 < s_2 < s_3$

$s_3 - s_2 = s_2 - s_1$

if using all calls:

$R = c_1 + c_3 - 2c_2$

if using all puts:

$R = p_1 + p_3 - 2p_2$

if using put bull spread and call bear spread:

$P = c_2 + p_2 - c_3 - p_1$

if using call bull spread and put bear spread:

$R = p_2 + c_2 - p_1 - c_3 - s_3 + s_2$

then

$P = s_3 - s_2 - R$ or $R = s_3 - s_2 - P$

$D = s_1 + R$

$U = s_3 - R$

Selling the Straddle

Another widely used options spreading technique is the straddle. It is applied when the investor feels there will be no great price fluctuations in the market.

The sale of a straddle is the simultaneous sale of both a put and a call with the same expiration date at the same strike price. This strategy is for the spreader who anticipates narrow price-range fluctuations in the market. For this strategy the spreader gets twice the profit that would have been made by writing a call or a put singularly. However, since the spreader reaps the reward, from both the call and the put, it also exposes the writer of the straddle to twice the risk.

Why? Let's suppose the straddle was written at July 50 for $1,000 ($500 for the put and $500 for the call), meaning a July expiration date and a $50 strike price. By selling both a put and a call, the writer establishes the same risk position as if selling both a call and a put separately.

If the market should rally in June and the stock in question were to rise to a point above 50, the buyer of the straddle would have established the right to buy the stock from the seller at 50 and sell the stock in the open market. In addition, the call buyer could sell his call in the secondary market for more than was originally paid.

Conversely, if the underlying stock of the straddle were to plummet, let us suppose to $35, then the straddle buyer could exercise his put and sell the stock at $50 and buy the stock back at $35 for a $15 profit (less trading costs).

The seller of the straddle embarks on this particular strategy with the expectation that there will be little or no movement in the stock being sold as a straddle, and of course the term "straddle" is simply derived from the writer or buyer having straddled or taken a position with respect to both a put and a call simultaneously.

SELL THE STRADDLE AND PURCHASE THE STOCK

The purchase of the stock allows its owner to take advantage of any upward price movement. However, with the sale of the straddle, the writer or seller buys limited downside protection by virtue of the premiums received for the puts and the calls. If the stock should go above the difference in the strike price and the premium paid to the straddle seller, then the seller would start to lose money. If the market should go downward significantly the seller could suffer a loss on the purchase stock side and the put side. The risk to the straddle seller at this point is the same as a covered call-writer purchasing on margin.

Reverse Option Hedge

The reverse option hedger thinks there will be dramatic movement in the market. Therefore, he buys two calls and sells short the stock. In order for this position to make money, the market will have to move enough upward or downward to recoup the cost of the two calls. The risk/reward ratio is similar to that of buying a straddle.

Volatility Spread

A spread which makes money if the stock moves up or down far and fast enough.

Diagonal Spread

A spread between options of the same class with different striking prices and expiration dates.

Combination Spread

Buying options at one strike price and expiration date and short options at a different exercise price and expiration date.

The Strangle

Simultaneously selling an out-of-the-money put and selling an out-of-the-money call. Or, simultaneously buying an out-of-the-money put and buying an out-of-the-money call.

The many aforementioned strategies demonstrate that if you have the bucks and the guts, options offer a shopper's bazaar of products. An investor can design an investment portfolio into virtually any risk/reward approach one might choose.

Be aware, however, that many of those pert, smart-looking yuppie brokers who will track you down, even to your vacation spot, to sell you the latest annuity may not understand what the possibilities of the options world are, much less be able to help you design a trading program to fit your risk/reward objectives. Don't let a fast-talking broker take you into uncharted water. As stated at the beginning of this chapter, these illustrations are meant as a show-and-tell demonstration rather than as a buy-and-serve recipe.

What thumping? . . . I didn't hear a noise . . . probably just your heart working, or the pounding of the surf below. Native drums? . . . I sure hope not. . . . Speaking of bad news, I almost forgot the biggest DON'T on Wall Street:

PIG (not now or *ever*)

P . . . Don't Panic.
I . . . Don't be Ignorant. Know what you are doing.
G . . . Don't get Greedy (just as pride goeth before a fall, greed precedes financial disaster).

NOMENCLATURE

"Don'ts" bring a new set of terms.

TO FALL OUT OF BED
the phrase used by Wall Streeters when a stock plummets

TOTAL RETURN CONCEPT
a covered call-selling strategy wherein the seller reaps profit as a result of the sum of capital gains, dividends, and options premiums rather than from each entity separately

SYNTHETIC POSITION
an equivalent stock position that is created by buying and selling options. For example, a synthetic put is

created by buying a call and simultaneously selling the stock short.

TO LIFT ONE LEG OF A SPREAD
to close one side of the spread out

PREMATURE ASSIGNMENT
when the writer of a call has the stock called away before expiration of its trading in-the-money

NONEVALUATION
the nonevaluation approach to determining the value of options is another school of thought that is not championed by the fair-value school of options evaluators. It calculates the difference in the percentage of the stock price change versus the percentage of change in the price of the option.

DOWNSIDE PROTECTION
a cushion which a stockowner acquires by selling a call to protect his investment should there be a decline in the stock price

INCREMENTAL RETURN CONCEPT
a strategy of covered call-writing wherein the owner of stock is seeking to earn additional income, even though he believes he will sell the stock for a higher price in the future

LOGNORMAL DISTRIBUTION
a method of statistical distribution used to analyze price movements in financial instruments

LETTER OF GUARANTEE

a document usually from a bank substantiating ownership of stock by a call seller. The letter will guarantee that the bank will deliver the customer's stock to the brokerage company if the call option is assigned.

MAINTENANCE MARGINS

Let's assume you already have a trading account and call up your stockbroker to buy 100 shares of XYZ at 50 per share on margin. The broker would ask that you send in $2,500 (half of $5,000) and make arrangements to lend you the remaining $2,500 to purchase the XYZ stock. This process is called buying on margin.

Buying listed options on margin is not permitted. However, if you were selling options instead of buying them, you would be asked by the brokerage house to put up money as a guarantee that you'd pay up in case the option sold was exercised by its buyer. This margin requirement may be in the form of cash or securities.

As mentioned earlier, one of the reasons you are cautioned against the more involved options strategies is the large amounts of capital outlay that these positions require.

Requirements are defined by the Federal Reserve Board under Regulation T. The brokerage firm, however, may establish stricter requirements for customers, but not less strict than Regulation T.

Margins on options are 30 percent of market value plus any in-the-money or minus any out-of-the-money amount. If the customer has received any premiums from the sale of options (as in the case of a conversion wherein you would sell a call), the brokerage firm may offset that amount received against the options requirement. And conversely, if the customer has paid premiums, those sums must be added to the requirement for the deposit.

Call example:

A customer sells an uncovered XYZ Jan 60 call at 6 when the market is 63. What is the margin requirement? Because the call is uncovered, .30 (percent) × 6300 = 1890 + 300 (the amount of in-the-money) = 2190 − 600 (premium received) = 1590.

Put example:

A customer sells an uncovered XYZ Oct 60 put at 6 when the market is 63. What is the margin requirement? .30 × 63 = 1890 − 300 (out-of-the-money amount) = 1590 − 600 = 990 (margin deposit).

You as a buyer of options may exercise as soon as ownership is confirmed. However, you are not likely to do so unless you find it more profitable than selling your option in the secondary market.

ROLLING OVER

buying back the option you previously sold and selling the same option with a different expiration date

WALKING DOWN

a strategy of selling calls against the decline in value of a stock position

Puff, puff . . . Hey! . . . look up there, the top of the crater . . . according to the map that ought to be it! That should do the trick.

13

FINER POINTS

Remember what I said about those sharp pencils and quick minds. . . .

ARBITRAGE

Arbitrage is the act of buying one asset and selling another in either the same or another market for a riskless profit. For example, an arbitrager might buy for 35 in one market and sell for 35¼ in another market.

This is the basic concept. However, one does not have to buy and sell the same asset, but rather create an equivalent to the position. For example, a combination of options and stocks could work out to be an equivalent position. The arbitrager spends a large part of his energies constructing positions that will bring profit with little or no risk.

In most cases the world of the arbitrager is closed to the general public: first, because of the speed with which the executions must take place; second, because the transaction costs are substantial. Arbitragers are usually independent floor traders or traders who work for firms that own the seats through which they trade, avoiding brokerage fees and thereby enjoying reduced transaction costs.

For a moment, step into the arbitrager's shoes. XYZ is trading at 46 and the XYZ Oct 40 call is trading at 5½. As an arbitrager you would:

1. Buy the call at 5½.
2. Sell the stock at 46.
3. Exercise the call to purchase ABC stock at 40.

You would profit 6 points (the difference between the market price of 46 and the strike price of 40), but you lose the 5½ points paid for the call.

What has happened in effect is that the arbitrager has bought the call at a discount. If the call was trading at parity, then the price of the call would have cost 6 rather than 5½.

The net result in this case was that you bought a call for 40 (strike price) plus 5½ (call premium), or 45½, and sold it for 46, making a profit of ½ point.

You may think ½ point isn't a lot, but consider how much you would make if you did this 10,000 times, as professional traders can afford to do. Substantial profits would start to mount.

A similar procedure can be followed using puts.

As an arbitrager let's say you buy XYZ stock at 42 and the Jan 55 put at 12¼. Then you exercise the put to sell the stock at 55. You make 13 points on this part of the transaction, but you lose the 12¼ that you pay for the put. Your net position is as follows:

Buy put at	12¼
Buy stock at	42
	54¼
Sell stock at	55
For a ¾ profit	

At parity the price of the put should have been 13.

Arbitrage opportunities will exist mostly when there are many deep-in-the-money options or when the option is near to expiration. Near the expiration date, the public interest in options will usually lessen, except in cases where they are buying to close out short positions. Many covered writers will allow their stock to be called away, thereby leaving the options markets to the arbitragers.

In most cases a larger market exists for stocks than for options. When the opposite is the case, however, the arbitrager would have to create an equivalent position by selling a call that is the numerical equivalent of the put; that is, selling at parity. For instance, if you could buy the Oct 40 call at 5½ but couldn't sell the stock at 46, instead you'd have to create a position by maybe selling an Oct 30 call at 16 (which would be the parity price): 30 + 16 = 46.

Similarly, you could create an equivalent position with puts.

You buy the Jan 55 put at 12¼, but find you can't buy the XYZ stock at 42. You could create a position by selling a Jun 70 put at 28 (which is priced at parity) for the same ¾-point profit.

CONVERSIONS

Another popular arbitrage technique is the process of converting a call into a put. In its most basic form a conversion is the combination of:

1. Selling a call, then
2. Buying the underlying stock, then
3. Buying a put

This position makes a profit if the total cost of the position is less than the striking price of the options.

If you did a conversion by buying the XYZ stock at 60, selling the XYZ Oct 55 call at 6½, and buying the XYZ Oct 55 put at 1, the total cost would be 54½ (60 for the stock plus put price of 1 minus 6½ received for the call). Since the difference between 54½ and the strike price of 55 is ½, the gross profit on the position would be ½ point. If it was necessary to carry the conversion for a month, you would have a carrying cost that would be deducted. Let us suppose the cost of carrying was ⅛ of a point per month; then the profit would be ½ of a point gross profit less ⅛ of a point, or ⅜ of a point net profit.

REVERSAL

A reversal is the opposite of a conversion. A reversal is profitable if the initial credit (sale price) is over the striking price of the option. In doing a reversal, you'd buy a 65 call at 2, sell stock at 60, sell 65 put for 7½. In a reversal the shorting of the stock may require that you pay out a dividend. If this is the case, and the dividend were to be $25 per hundred shares, the dividend of $25 would then be deducted from the ½-point gross profit of the reversal to arrive at the net profit of ¼ point.

DIVIDEND ARBITRAGE

When a dividend is announced, it causes the price of the put to increase by the amount of the dividend and causes the call to decrease, usually because of the drop in price of the underlying stock.

Theoretically, the day before a stock goes ex-dividend, the time value of all puts should equal at least the dividend amount. For example, if the dividend is $1, then the value of this $1 should be reflected in the put's price. There is a type of dividend arbitrage possible from this phenomenon in the marketplace.

If XYZ closes at 50 and is going ex-dividend by 1 on the following day, theoretically a 55 put should trade for 6 points (the amount of the in-the-money plus the $1 of the dividend) and the stock should open at 49, which is 6 points in-the-money. If the time value of the put is trading at a discount of 5½, the riskless profit netted by the arbitrager is ½ point. You would:

1. Buy the put at 5½.
2. Buy the stock at 50.
3. Hold the put for the 1 (when the stock goes ex-dividend).
4. Exercise the put to sell the stock at 55.

You would make the difference between buying the stock at 50 and selling it at 55 (= 5 points) plus 1 point dividend. Since, however, you would lose 5½ (the cost of buying the put), you would make ½ point as net profit.

CARRYING COSTS

When the trader purchases his 500, or even 10,000, shares of stock, where does the money come from? Probably not out of his vault, passbook savings, or money market account, but rather from some lending institution that charges for the use of the money (this is an opportunity cost because that money could be doing something else). Large traders often have lending arrangements with an institution, the rationale being that when possible, it is better to use other people's money to make money with. The cost of carrying a position reflects the interest charged on the borrowed money and is called a carrying cost. If the rate of lending were 12 percent per annum, the monthly charge for carrying a position would be at 1 percent per month.

If, for example, a position is expected to pay a 3

percent gross profit over a two-month period, and the carrying costs are 1 percent per month, the 3 percent gross profit will have to be reduced by the 1 percent borrowing cost times two months (=2%), to arrive at a 1 percent net profit. Therefore, interest rates can be important in determining to what extent a trade will be profitable. If, for example, a trader can borrow money at a lower rate than can his competitors, he may be able to sell for less and realize a greater profit.

Interest rates are so important that the government through the Treasury Department and the Federal Reserve can send ripples of fear down Wall Street with impending notice of an interest-rate change of even ½ or 1 percent.

For instance, if the federal government should decide to make less money available in the economy, theoretically, according to the principles of supply and demand, interest rates would go higher. If the supply of X becomes less and the demand for that X remains constant, the result will be that the price of X will rise, which might mean that instead of borrowing to buy stocks, investors may choose to sell stocks and put their monies into what they think will be higher yielding investments. This would push the market downward and make puts more valuable. If, however, on the other hand, the government caused a lot of money to be available (causing lower interest rates), owners of stocks might be willing to borrow and buy more stocks, thus causing the market to rise and the value of calls to increase. Another scenario might occur if the President decided to give in to the rumblings of foreign exporters and caused the devaluation of the dollar. In this case investors would most probably sell the dollar and put their money into something they felt was more inherently valuable, like precious metals (i.e., gold and silver), thereby sending gold and silver prices upward and increasing the value of gold call options and probably depressing stock options.

Note that I have prefaced my prediction of what the markets may or may not do in relation to interest rates with a big MAYBE. . . . I do so because many modern economists have been beating their brains out, tying their tongues up, and crucifying their calculators for a long time now all in the name of studying this ever-changing phenomenon called interest rates in hopes of discovering some patterns of predictable behavior, yet it still proves to be an elusive butterfly.

Traders are well aware of how interest rates work and have even devised clever games to take advantage of the small difference in interest rates between countries. For example, in what is called interest-rate arbitrage, a trader can (1) take U.S. dollars and exchange them for a foreign currency, (2) take that foreign currency and invest it in an interest-bearing instrument (payable in the future, a 90-day commercial instrument, for example), and (3) sell a futures contract to hedge the potential drop in price of the foreign currency relative to U.S. dollars. This can lead to profits if it is done correctly.

Everything has a cost, and money is no exception. Banks charge traders and large companies for the use of money the same way they charge individuals, and from the borrower's standpoint, the goal is always the same—to negotiate the lowest possible rate. So, as you develop in your investment program, keep in mind that borrowing carries with it a cost and should be treated like an unlabeled medicine bottle—*Handle with Care*.

As an options buyer you will ultimately be faced with profits or losses. The extent of these profits and losses will necessarily be tied to both commissions and taxes.

Yes, I said taxes, the grandnephew of the Grim Reaper himself, who in the end seems destined to get us all.

TAXES

With each gain or loss you experience, you will be faced with having that gain or loss considered for tax purposes. In tax language those gains or losses will be considered either short- or long-term.

Much concern is given to short-term or long-term taxation because of its effect on your real profit. Remember this: Short-term gains are taxed at a higher rate.

If you experienced a short-term gain of $100 and you were in a 25 percent tax bracket, you'd pay .25 × $100 = $25. However, if you experienced a long-term gain of $100, and you were in a 25 percent tax bracket, you'd pay .25 × $40 = $10, a saving of 2/5, or 40 percent.

So obviously, the game rules expand to try to create as many long-term gain situations as possible. But wait . . . there is something called the Internal Revenue Service standing in the way with rules and regulations regarding what can be considered long-term or short-term gains.

Short-term gains or losses on options are considered those the buyer or seller holds for six months or under, and long-term gains or losses are those that are held for more than six months.

As mentioned earlier, the options position can be terminated by:

1. Trading in a secondary market
2. Exercise
3. Expiration

When you buy an option, to determine capital gain or loss, the formula is:

Net proceeds of sale − adjusted cost of acquisition (ACA) = gain or loss

Note both net proceeds and ACA should reflect commission costs. For example: If you buy an S&P 100 Oct 160 call at 4 and sell it at 7, deduct transaction costs of $50.

Net Proceeds	minus	ACA	equals	Gain
700(25) = 675	−	400(25) = 425	=	250

Or on the other hand, you bought at 400 and sold at 300, less transaction costs of $50.

Net Proceeds	minus	ACA	equals	Loss
300(25) = 275	−	400(25) = 425	=	150

Both transactions would be considered short-term loss or gain.

EXERCISE. If you bought an Oct 50 call at 3 on March 10 and on June 10 you exercise and sell for 56, you'd have paid:

Net Proceeds minus	ACA	Gain
5600 − (stock) −	50 + (call premium) 3 = 5300	300

EXPIRATION. If you bought a put or call and it expired worthless, your loss would be the amount of the premium plus commission. If the premium was 400 and transaction costs were 25:

Net Proceeds minus	ACA	Loss (Short-Term)
0 −	400(25) = 425	425

If you owned the underlying stock, the situation would be more complicated.

If you bought a put to hedge your long stock position, the purchase of the put would wipe out the holding period of your owning the underlying stock if you owned it for less than six months, and thus any profit you might realize would be treated as a short-term gain. The holding period would not begin again until after the put was disposed of.

However, if you had owned the underlying stock for more than six months, the purchase of the put would not affect the holding period of the underlying stock. This falls under the "short-sale rule." However, if when you bought the underlying stock you purchased the put simultaneously with the known intent that the put would hedge your long stock position, the transaction could qualify as a "married" transaction and be eligible for long-term tax status.

Note: There are many more varied and complex strategies involving taxes and options. However, the best possible advice to you the options buyer is to find someone who knows and understands the tax ramifications of the money machinations available in options trading. As the laws are continually changing, options contracts are also subject to change; therefore the investor is best off under the guidance of someone continually dealing with the changes in both areas.

Arbitrage, conversions, carrying costs, taxes, notwithstanding, never forget, a major key to success is to remain alert and have the courage and flexibility to act quickly on the opportunities that you may ferret out. Some dormant stock may suddenly heat up, sparking activity in the option of that stock, or some narrow-based index, for example, the oil option index, responding to a shift in the always volatile mideastern situation may suddenly allow you (the observant early bird) an opportunity to make a killing.

Look! Just like the map said! See down there over the rim . . . there's the clearing, there's the tree . . . and the rock must be where the treasure is buried. From here on you will have to go it alone. . . . Good-bye. . . . Here's the shovel. Good luck. . . .

14

GERONIMO

Not ready to leave the nest? Sure you are . . . you have studied the map, the Mists, the Game, even the gauntlet, and the odds hold no secrets for you.

In the back of his book *Creating Wealth* Robert Allen quotes a wonderful excerpt from the French poet Apollinaire.

> *Come to the edge, He said.*
> *They said, We are afraid.*
> *Come to the edge, He said.*
> *They came,*
> *He pushed them . . . and they flew.*

Still a little leery about the distances from the branch (hypothetical) down to the ground (reality), huh? How about a dry-run flight with me . . . Maybe you can pick up some last-minute tips before you try your wings.

How about a little preflight briefing?

Remember, easy does it. All the books and courses ever invented can't replace actual experience. However, with a little trick called paper trading we can approximate the real world. To paper-trade is to pick an option to trade, in your head, then take all the steps exactly as you would if you had actually put down your money, except you don't. When paper trading, you should follow through with mock liquidations of your position including the calculation of commission, profits and loss, everything. The more conscientiously and often you test the wind this way, the better prepared you will be for the big day. Even when you paper-trade, there will be times when you lose, but a loss does not mean that you have necessarily made a stupid error. The trick is to earn more—much more is better—than you lose. To play the Options Game and think you will never stumble is as unrealistic as a fighter, championship class or not, climbing into the ring believing he is not going to have a glove laid on him. Like a boxer, a speculator is going to catch some punches, too. Options are going to be fun just like I promised you. Still, you have to take a sock now and then. That's where the Stamina, Concentration, and Sense of Humor that I said you were going to need come in.

On paper you may try trading any volume you wish. But when you decide to step up to using real money, no more than five contracts at a time should be the rule. A brokerage house will generally give you cheaper rates if you do volume business. Don't take the bait—wait. Even though they say:

"*Bought sense be the best sense*" (Southern axiom)

. . . Why learn the hard way?

Possession may be 90 percent of the law, but survival is 100 percent, the whole shebang. Rule one in options is to stay in the game, and you can't stay in it if you blow your bankroll, so start small and go slow.

Stay humble. The market is tougher than you. Don't get cocky if you happen to get in a lucky trade or two. When the market talks, it pays to listen. Think of the market as a nine-foot, two-thousand-pound gorilla. You don't tell the market anything . . . the market tells you.

A fascinating thing about the financial community is that the very same news, depending on how one reads the leaves, seems to foretell to various people (different swings of the keel) different market directions. Identical information can generate diametrically opposed reactions. Interest rates are lowered, for example . . . Some might feel that because rates are falling, people will switch from bonds to stocks, and stock prices will go *up*, whereas another faction may feel that since interest rates are lower, it is an indication of a weak economy and therefore owners of stock, based on the thinking that earnings will be falling, will sell and stocks will go *down*, not *up*.

Although most beginners tend to look for only potential winners, the game has two sides. There can be big profits in picking losers, too. Our buy-only strategy doesn't limit you to only the rising side of the market.

Don't forget there are puts in your arsenal as well as calls.

Keep it simple. Fancy dips, dives, and rolls are not for serious business. Keeping it uncomplicated doesn't make you a jerk. Believe me, if I had a worm for every bird who ever outsmarted himself with some convoluted laborious strategy, I would never have to work again. Don't try to chase too many stocks at once either. The buy-only strategy, and trading options in just one stock, is the best way to begin.

The majority of money-makers (not just beginners either) keep it as simple as possible. Try to stick to your plan and avoid getting caught up in the momentum.

In picking an option choose a listed one rather than an over-the-counter one. Whenever possible, trade options in stocks that are related to things that are naturally interesting to you. If you have a feel for a certain product, it will enhance your insight about its probable performance. Call it intuition if you will, but often a casual observation by, say, the wife or kid can be a valuable clue as to how a new product will do.

If you happen to get lucky and find an option whose price is being affected by either unusually good news or bad news, then you could try the "anti-herd" approach. For some long-lost or yet-to-be-discovered reason people have an overwhelming tendency to follow the crowd, an uncontrollable abdication of individuality to the mass mentality called herd instinct. This is a "group-think" psychology that brings crowds to react and overreact to the same thing, oftentimes with disastrous results. History is littered with cases of the mass-psychology phenomenon, and even though people say they know better, there are more rules than exceptions.

In recognition of this tendency you might adopt the contrarian approach; this boils down to, when there is terrifically good news about a stock and everyone thinks the price will go up forever, buy a put. On the other hand, if a report of bad news has just sent a stock crashing, buy a call. When the stock reverses its direction and you are into profit, liquidate your position.

If nothing spectacular is happening, you can always try the "go with the herd" approach and do some charting. Look up the closing prices of a stock for the last fifteen days. Then start keeping a moving fifteen-day average of that stock. Keeping a moving average consists of adding the closing prices and dividing by 15. Each day you add the newest closing price and simply drop the oldest.

Investment advisers who chart stocks often use moving averages with a longer time span—two months to a half year or even more. But remember, an option is a wasting asset, a sort of perishable stock. As an options speculator it is advisable to use the shorter time span.

Stocks tend to have lulls, then periods of activity. That is the reason you wait until the stock breaks out of the fifteen-day moving average before you buy the option. There is no need to own the option with its time value eroding under you for months, waiting for a burst of volatility.

If the stock goes above the fifteen-day moving average, buy a call option. If it goes below, buy the put. The time to liquidate the option that you bought is when the price breaks back through in the opposite direction.

The theory behind buying the call option if the stock breaks the moving average on the upside (or the put if it goes below) is that if you are right, the stock will continue to go up, increasing the call option's value. The moment the stock reverses itself you should get out quickly. The getting out when the stock goes against you fosters discipline. It disciplines you into cutting your losses if the stock reverses itself too soon (before your premium and commission costs have been recouped); or, on the other hand if the stock has moved enough in your favor to make the option profitable, before the tide turns, it disciplines you into taking your winnings before there is a chance of your getting wiped out.

Loyalty is not a moral plus when it comes to options. It is your business to anticipate the market, but don't let a hunch become an immovable opinion. Abandon ship when you have to.

. . . It's time to fly. . . . Lookee, here's a nice limb, the best branch on the whole tree. . . . Ready? . . . You'll be fine. Nothing like having a good jumping-off place (no pun intended), they say.

Okay? Now, remember, never be a Pig. Don't panic, don't be ignorant, and don't get greedy, and watch out for the MISTS OF MOOLAH.

Here we go. Ready? One, two . . . *three*!

EPILOGUE

IF

If you can keep your head when all about you
Are losing theirs and blaming it on you;
If you can trust yourself when all men doubt you,
But make allowance for their doubting too;
If you can wait and not be tired by waiting,
Or being lied about, don't deal in lies,
Or, being hated, don't give way to hating,
And yet don't look too good, nor talk too wise;

If you can dream—and not make dreams your master;
If you can think and not make thoughts your aim;
If you can meet with triumph and disaster
And treat those two imposters just the same;

If you can bear to hear the truth you've spoken
Twisted by knaves to make a trap for fools,
Or watch the things you gave your life to broken,
And stoop and build 'em up with wornout tools

If you can make one heap
Of all your winnings,
And risk it on one turn of pitch-and-toss,
And lose, and start again at your beginnings
And never breathe a word about your loss;
If you can force your heart and nerve and sinew
To serve your turn long after they are gone,
And so hold on when there is nothing in you
Except the Will which says to them: "Hold on";

If you can talk with crowds, and keep your virtue,
Or walk with kings—nor lose the common touch;
If neither foes nor loving friends can hurt you;
If all men count with you, but none too much;
If you can fill the unforgiving minute
With sixty seconds' worth of distance run—
Yours is the Earth and everything that's in it,
And—which is more—you'll be a Man, my son!***

—Rudyard Kipling

*(or Woman)
**(or daughter)

SELECTED BIBLIOGRAPHY

Tennyson said, "We are part of all that we have met. . . ." The following are a few of the books that have furnished me clues.

SPECIFICS (Options)

The Stock Options Manual. Gary L. Gastineau. New York Institute of Finance, 1975.

Just what the title says, a manual from A to Z on options. Although it is slightly out-of-date (it does not treat index options), its treatment of fundamentals makes it a must for a speculator's options library.

Options as a Strategic Investment. Lawrence G. McMillan. New York Institute of Finance, 1980.

A serious options player's guide. Intense reading, offering an endless menu of strategies.

Sure Thing Options Trading. George Angell. Doubleday & Co., 1983.

An informative read on the what, who, when, where, and how of listed options in straightforward digestible language.

Exchange publications.

Each exchange and the OCC (Options Clearing Corporation) have helpful up-to-the-minute publications which can be obtained from your broker or by writing the respective exchanges. For example, the Amex's *A Guide to Listed Options* offers a useful discussion of the basics.

GENERAL (Wall Street)

The Traders. Sonny Kleinfield. Holt, Reinhart & Winston, 1983.

A close-up profile of traders. It not only captures the traders' physical world blow by blow but also explores the psychologies that motivate the subjects.

Favorable Executions: The Wall Street Specialist and the Auction Market. Michael G. Zahorchak. Van Nostrand Reinhold, 1974.

Worth the effort for the glimpse it offers into the specialist's mind and the intricacies of Wall Street.

Understanding Wall Street. Jeffrey B. Little and Lucien Rhodes. Liberty Publishing, 1978.

A clear concise explanation of the principles and mechanics that make up Wall Street. A good primer.

The Wall Street Jungle. Richard Ney. Grove Press, 1970.

An entertaining book that shows you why the rich stay rich, by going behind the scenes to describe and expose how and why the stock market works the way it does.

The Tao Jones Average. Bennett W. Goodspeed. Penguin Books; first published by E. P. Dutton, 1983.

Wall Street seen through the eyes of an Eastern philosophy. Quirky, whimsical, and with brilliant flashes.

Money Makes Money and the Money Money Makes Makes More Money. G. Krefetz and R. Marossi. World Publishing Co., 1970.

A wry look at how some have been able to do it. The implications are fascinating.

Contrarian Investment Strategy. David Dreman. Random House, 1979.

The contrarian manifesto, simultaneously solid and feisty, a clever investment approach that teaches the reader to forge ahead with courage against the conventional one.

The Money Market: Myth, Reality and Practice. Maricia Stigum. Dow Jones Irwin, 1978.

A bible of financial instruments. It explains the commandments as well as the where-art-thous of the money marketplace from banks to bonds to brokers and all the green stuff in between.

The Art of Speculation. Philip Carret. Fraser Publishing Co., 1979.

Wall Street before computer technology. The methods have changed, and the moves are faster, but it's still the same old game.

How to Make Your Money Make Money. Edited by Arthur Levitt, Jr. Dow Jones Irwin, 1981.

A series of papers by our captains of economy, surveying investment possibilities ranging from antiques to tax shelters.

MISCELLANEOUS (life)

The Alpha Strategy. John A. Pugsley. Stratford Press, 1980.

A novel, iconoclastic approach to economics based on what purports to be an everyman commonsense point of view. Provocative, grumpy, and fun.

Economics Deciphered: A Layman's Survival Guide. Maurice Levi. Basic Books, 1981.

A down-to-earth explanation of why money acts the way it does. However, the deciphering starts in second gear rather than from zero.

Commodity Options. Terry Mayer. New York Institute of Finance. 1983.

Just what the subtitle claims it is, A User's Guide to Speculating and Hedging. A windfall to all who care to specialize in commodity options.

Bad Money. L. J. Davis. St. Martin's Press, 1983.
A candid look at how big money can fall into the pot and come up smelling like a rose.

Paper Money. Adam Smith. Summit Books, 1980.
A little name-dropping, a little gossip, a little information, and a lot of gab. More cocktail chatter than money.

*The Holy Bible**
The source of the quote "the love of money is the root of all evil" (1 Tim. 6:10).

Megatrends. John Naisbitt. Warner Books, 1982.
An insightful trendy read on our changing society. Raises important questions about the future despite itself.

Understanding Media. Marshall McLuhan. Mentor Books, 1964.
A thought-provoking theorization of how and why the media does what it does to us. Even when the book is esoteric it's interesting.

The Theory of the Leisure Class. Thorstein Veblen. 1899; Viking Press, 1975.
Commentaries on the sociopolitical ramifications of wealth. The chapter on Conspicuous Consumption is a classic.

Creating Wealth. Robert G. Allen. Simon & Schuster, 1983.

*Title copyrighted 1979 by some smart guy.

One man's opinion of the road to riches. Part inspiration, part placebo, most interesting between the lines.

In Search of Excellence. Thomas J. Peters and Robert H. Waterman, Jr. Warner Books, 1982.

A lesson in what keeps some corporations running in the black. Lots of facts, figures, and observations.

Wisconsin Death Trip. Michael Lesy. Pantheon Books, 1973.

The cantankerous side of human nature, as seen through the pages of a small-town newspaper before the turn of the century. Disturbing and edifying.

INDEX